SINGAPORE
PERSPECTIVES
Singapore.World

SINGAPORE
PERSPECTIVES
Singapore.World

Edited by
Ariel Tan
Andrew Lim
Rachel Hau
Institute of Policy Studies, Singapore

Published by

World Scientific Publishing Co. Pte. Ltd.

5 Toh Tuck Link, Singapore 596224

USA office: 27 Warren Street, Suite 401-402, Hackensack, NJ 07601

UK office: 57 Shelton Street, Covent Garden, London WC2H 9HE

British Library Cataloguing-in-Publication Data
A catalogue record for this book is available from the British Library.

SINGAPORE PERSPECTIVES
Singapore.World

Copyright © 2019 by Institute of Policy Studies (IPS)

All rights reserved.

ISBN 978-981-120-742-6
ISBN 978-981-120-478-4 (pbk)

For any available supplementary material, please visit
https://www.worldscientific.com/worldscibooks/10.1142/11399#t=suppl

Desk Editor: Sandhya Venkatesh

Contents

About This Book

The Institute of Policy Studies (IPS) held its annual flagship conference, Singapore Perspectives, on 28 January 2019 at the Sands Expo and Convention Centre at Marina Bay Sands. It brought together 1,200 attendees from the public and private sectors, and civil society.

Themed "Singapore.World", the conference focused on recent geopolitical developments, their trajectory over the coming years and their implications for Singapore and the region.

Conference Concept

OVERVIEW

The post-Cold War world order is undergoing significant disruptions and headed towards prolonged uncertainty. This is primarily driven by the dynamics of strategic competition and engagement between the United States (US), the predominant power, and China, the rising power. Both powers are contending with deep issues of national identity and purpose. The US and Chinese leaderships have raised fundamental questions about the current world order, and their respective roles, rights and obligations vis-à-vis the international system.

Arguably, the world order and open trading system have been fraying at the seams for some time. Regimes that flout international norms have not been brought to account. Trade has lifted millions out of poverty, but also caused severe economic dislocation for workers. Questions are being asked about the benefits and costs of globalisation across the world. Populist nationalism, with the attendant attractions of protectionism and rejection of multilateralism and international law and treaties, could increasingly be brought to bear on the foreign policy of key states.

To complicate but also ameliorate this complex state of affairs, the US and China, together with the rest of the world, are much more integrated today than during the Cold War, with dense and entangled networks of economic production and exchange, and information and people flows. This is powered by technological advances that are accelerating beyond the understanding of most individuals or organisations. There remain important areas of shared concern — for instance, the proliferation of weapons of mass destruction, terrorism, international financial stability and climate change. These issues should promote cooperation but may also become sources of friction.

What are the implications for small states like Singapore and countries in Southeast Asia? If effective statecraft is to mobilise all national resources necessary to preserve a nation's sovereignty, security and prosperity, how should countries respond to these geopolitical, economic and technological challenges? Challenges to state sovereignty now extend beyond the military and political, to indirect and deniable influence via individuals, communities, business and cyberspace.

How should Singapore and Southeast Asia respond and work together among themselves and with partners beyond? What must Singaporeans understand about this changing world, and how can they do their part?

SESSION I: SINGAPORE AND THE WORLD

Chinese President Xi Jinping has reportedly said that China will reach its goal of becoming "a global leader in terms of composite national strength and international influence" by 2050. He has also offered China's development model as a new option for other countries. US President Donald Trump, on the other hand, has put US allies in Asia and Europe on notice that there will be a review of their partnership and role. He withdrew the US from the Trans-Pacific Partnership (TPP) after his inauguration, in fulfilment of his campaign pledge, and has characterised China as taking actions inimical to US interests both within the US and elsewhere. China has responded to US challenges by stating that it will stand firm while keeping its door open for negotiations. Observers argue that we are not just witnessing a trade war but a prolonged period of strategic competition and potential crisis.

Contending with the ups and downs of US-China relations has been the core business of statecraft for states in the Asia Pacific region since the start of the 21st century. What is new? What are the long-term structural shifts in power that we should watch out for?

How well has Singapore dealt with the US and China, and how must it change and adapt its posture to meet current and future challenges? What is the long-term perspective it should take? Is Singapore society organised and resilient enough to meet these challenges resolutely? What do Singaporeans need to understand?

SESSION II: SINGAPORE AND INTERNATIONAL ECONOMICS

The United States still dominates the global economy, although its share of world GDP fell to 24.32 per cent while China's rose to 14.84 per cent in 2017. According to the World Bank, China's Belt and Road Initiative (BRI) is a historic transcontinental initiative that aims to connect China to some 65 other countries that account for over 30 per cent of global GDP, 62 per cent of the world's population and 75 per cent of known energy reserves. At the same time, the US economy has experienced healthy growth in recent years. It remains a competitive, adaptive and innovative economy that is attractive to international talent and investment.

If political and economic competition intensifies in the coming years, what are the implications for the international financial and trading system? An open trading system has benefitted trading nations like Singapore that are plugged into the global supply chains that bring capital and technological know-how. Singapore is a shipping, air, and financial and business hub for more than 37,000 companies from across the world, including 7,000 multinational companies. It is a key financing services centre for BRI projects and supports the internationalisation of the renminbi, being one of two Asian countries that are part of the Renminbi Qualified Foreign Institutional Investor programme (the other being the Republic of Korea).

How can Singapore and Southeast Asian countries work together to face the headwinds and capitalise on new opportunities? What is the future of Singapore's hub strategy? How should it adjust its international economic strategy and national socioeconomic policies?

Finally, how can Singapore encourage an optimistic and cosmopolitan mindset among Singaporeans towards the region and the rest of the world, to nurture its own workforce, welcome international talent, and encourage Singaporeans to venture into the region and beyond for learning and business opportunities?

SESSION III: SINGAPORE AND THE REGION

Japan, Korea, India, Australia, countries in Southeast Asia, and ASEAN as a whole are likely to face increasing pressures from US-China rivalry. The US has strong alliances with many of these countries and has demonstrated its interest in the South China Sea dispute, but its other moves, like withdrawing from the TPP, have raised concerns about prospects for long-term US influence in the region. China has sought to deepen its political and economic ties with countries in the region, proposing historic and far-reaching initiatives like the Belt and Road Initiative and the Asian Infrastructure Investment Bank. US-China competition for dominance and influence is likely to grow in the coming years.[1]

Southeast Asian states are witnessing significant political flux domestically, particularly as their economies mature and undergo restructuring; all are eager for foreign investment and trade with external partners. While there are shades of differences in their interests and relations with the major powers, ASEAN member states share the common goal of security and prosperity, and have generally managed to forge a common position in the past five decades. However, their continued ability to do so as a united and key player in regional affairs has been brought into question in recent years.

Governments and non-government organisations and groups will also need to assess current efforts to promote a sense of community and shared

---

[1] According to the fourth wave of the Asian Barometer Survey in East Asia, conducted from June 2014 to June 2016, the US is very well regarded in most of the countries in Asia, save for Malaysia (50 per cent have a positive view of the US) and Indonesia (45 per cent). However, China is generally perceived to have greater regional influence than the US. To the question of which country has the most influence in Asia now, the response in each of the following countries is: **Vietnam** (China 60 per cent vs US 18 per cent); **Japan** (61 vs 27); **Singapore** (54 vs 29); **China** (58 vs 28); **Korea** (67 vs 25); **Thailand** (49 vs 19); **Malaysia** (42 vs 46); **Cambodia** (27 vs 46); **Indonesia** (37 vs 37); the **Philippines** (22 vs 59); and **Myanmar** (57 vs 32). Source: Chu Yun-han, Chang Yu-tzung, and Huang Min-hua (2016). *How East Asians View the Influence of United States vs a Rising China*. Presented at the Brookings Institution's conference on competition over soft power in East Asia, Washington DC, 29 September 2016.
Retrieved from: www.asianbarometer.org/pdf/Brookings2016.pdf.

interests among the citizens of ASEAN, and to make a real push towards this goal.

What are the potential flashpoints that will have serious security and economic implications for Southeast Asia? What would be the likely alignment of interests and outcomes? How can Singapore and its ASEAN brethren forge unity to protect their continued security, prosperity, and freedom and independence of action?

Introduction by
Janadas Devan[1]

Today, 28 January 2019, is the bicentennial of Stamford Raffles' arrival in Singapore. His own and other accounts have his ship, the *Indiana*, and its accompanying schooner, *Enterprise*, anchoring off St John's Island at 4pm 200 years ago today — just in time for tea, I presume. A delegation from Singapore boarded the *Indiana* the same afternoon, curious what Raffles and his crew were about. Raffles asked them if the Dutch — then Britain's chief rival for supremacy in this region — were present on the main island of Singapore. Told the Dutch were not, Raffles landed on the main island — by some accounts on the evening of 28 January itself, by others the morning of 29 January. This evening, 200 years later, the Prime Minister will be launching the Singapore Bicentennial commemorations at the Asian Civilisations Museum, near the spot where Raffles, Farquhar and their crew first landed on our island. The Union Jack was officially raised on 6 February 1819, following the signing of the Singapore Treaty between Raffles and Sultan Hussein and his Temenggong.

For better or worse, that moment marked a decisive break for this island. Singapore had a past before Raffles landed here — a past stretching back at least to the 13th century. The gentleman-pirate did not find or found Singapore, as the British once claimed, as though nobody knew of its existence till Raffles stumbled upon it. But the British arrival here did lead to a future vastly different — unimaginably so — from the preceding 500 years. There are many ways that decisive break can be understood. Most obviously,

---

[1] This version has been edited by IPS for the purposes of inclusion in this publication. Mr Devan's full remarks are available in video format on the IPS website.

it marked the entrenchment of colonialism in the Malayan peninsula. Singapore became a part of the British Empire — a pawn in the prosecution of its interests in China, for example, in the opium trade, and later, in the early 20th century, as a naval outpost to defend the eastern approaches to British India, the jewel in the crown. We were never of interest to Britain only for ourselves. We were of value only as part of the constellation of intricately intertwined interests that constituted the British Empire — the most far-flung empire in human history, an empire on which it was famously said the sun never set.

But I wish to propose this morning another way of understanding 1819. Raffles' arrival, unbeknown to himself, marked the explosive eruption of modernity in this part of the world. Now modernity is not new. There have been many modernities in history. The modernity I speak of is the trajectory that led to the present, with Singapore as a "global city", as Mr S Rajaratnam forecast with great prescience we would be. His speech of 46 years ago, in 1972, provides a useful frame for me to outline the various possible themes of this conference, "Singapore.World".

As Rajaratnam pointed out, the concept of a "global city" was first formulated by the historian Arnold Toynbee. It was a new form of human organisation and settlement, Toynbee had argued. Cities of the past were relatively isolated centres of local civilisations and regional empires. "They were either capital cities or cities of prestige, holy cities, city states and even capitals of convenience." The global city, by contrast, was an "Ecumenopolis" — a world-embracing if not world-straddling entity. This is how Rajaratnam saw it:

> The Global Cities, unlike earlier cities, are linked intimately with one another. Because they are more alike they reach out to one another through the tentacles of technology. Linked together they form a chain of cities which today shape and direct, in varying degrees of importance, a world-wide system of economics. It is my contention that Singapore is becoming a component of that system — not a major component but a growingly important one.

This was in 1972. Today, we have indeed become "a major component" in this system of linked global cities, a world-embracing "Ecumenopolis". Forty-six years later, what might we say of Rajaratnam's vision? Can our future still be said to be encompassed in being a node in a system of linked global cities: New York and Shanghai, London and Berlin, Tokyo and Paris, Hong Kong and Singapore? How has the vision of Singapore as a global city held up?

To begin with, the vision has held up remarkably well. Indeed, Rajaratnam's speech might be regarded as one of the founding documents of independent Singapore, on par almost with the Separation Agreement. Why do I say that? Because prior to this speech, we did not have a theory — a "story", as we would say now — as to how Singapore, alone and bereft of a hinterland, might not only survive but also thrive. Perhaps only a couple of you here would remember this, but Rajaratnam's 1972 speech began with a question: How come, seven years after separating from Malaysia, Singapore is still surviving? After all, all our founding leaders, especially Rajaratnam, had assumed "an independent Singapore cannot be viable," as he himself admits in his speech. The settled conviction then, on both sides of the Causeway, was that "a small city state, without a natural hinterland, without a large domestic market and no raw materials to speak of, has a near-zero chance of survival politically, economically or militarily." So why did we not sue, on bended knees, to be readmitted into Malaysia, as the Tunku and other Malaysian leaders had expected us to?

Rajaratnam's answer — and this was the first time it was articulated explicitly thus — was that Singapore could defy the odds because it had begun transforming itself into a new kind of city, a global city, with the world as its market. Before we had assumed Singapore could at best be a regional city — playing the role of a middleman as exemplified by our dependence on entrepôt trade. Its transformation into a global city, with the world as its hinterland, was what enabled Singapore to prosper despite the loss of a common market with Malaysia.

(Incidentally, though Rajaratnam was the first to articulate this vision of Singapore as a global city, it was Dr Albert Winsemius — the Dutchman who fortuitously did come often to Singapore roughly 150 years after Raffles was relieved to find no Dutchman here — it was Winsemius who first told our founding leaders that the world could be our market. Visiting Singapore soon after Separation and discovering Mr Lee Kuan Yew, Dr Goh Keng Swee and the rest staring up at the ceiling in despair, wondering how we were to survive without a hinterland, Winsemius told them to stop moaning. Why are you worried about the loss of a common market of a mere 10 million, he asked them, when the whole world beckons? We take all these insights for granted now but they were once unthought of — perhaps even unthinkable. The received wisdom in development economics then stressed import substitution and producing for protected markets.)

My second observation is that Rajaratnam's forecast of how our economy, along with the global economy, would develop was spot on. He did not use the term "global supply chain" but that is what he meant when he spoke of the "internationalisation of production" led by multinational corporations. Nor did he speak of "globalisation" — another term that was not current as yet in the 1970s — but that is what he was gesturing towards when he observed: "The conventional idea that goods move internationally but that factors of production do not is being eroded by new realities."

But do cities — global cities, to be precise — remain the primary engines of the global economy? I do not have time, let alone the qualifications, to pronounce at length or authoritatively on this subject, but the ecology of cities, I suspect, is more complicated now. Global cities undoubtedly remain prominent in that ecology. But we also have a plethora of regional cities, manufacturing centres like Shenzhen, financial centres like Zurich, technology and innovation constellations like Silicon Valley, hubs of various kinds, satellites and triangles and what not.

In addition, globalisation has eroded the distinctions between cities and countries, regions and the globe. Singapore need no longer wrestle with a choice: Either we remain a regional city, serving our immediate neighbourhood, as we did for almost 150 years, or we leapfrog the region to hook up with a network of other global cities, as was the main (but by no means exclusive) thrust of our economy for the past 50 years.

Our region, like many other regions, has itself been absorbed into the global supply chain. As a result, our economy can be at once global as well as regional. With the global centre of gravity shifting to Asia, we can pursue what has been called a Global-Asia strategy, with Singapore serving as a gateway to the world for Asia and a gateway to Asia for the world — reprising our historic entrepôt or intermediation role but on a vaster, more complicated, more interdependent stage.

Rajaratnam's vision of Singapore as a global city has come to pass not least because the first 50 years of our existence as an independent, sovereign city-state coincided with a particularly benign period in world history. We could not have guessed it in 1965, when the Vietnam War was still raging and Mao's China was in the throes of that mad paroxysm known as the Cultural Revolution. But the second half of the 20th century saw the greatest expansion of trade the world has ever seen, as barriers to the free movement of goods, services, capital, talents, ideas and innovations crumbled and the primarily Anglo-Saxon liberal world order triumphed.

Which leads me to the third observation: Is that world order retreating, as many fear? And if it is, how is Singapore to position itself? These are questions Rajaratnam was not unaware of. For in that same speech, he spoke of the possibility of this global system collapsing:

> ...Singapore survives and will survive because it has established a relationship of interdependence in the rapidly expanding global economic system. Singapore's economic future will, as the years go by, become more and more rooted in this global system. It will grow and prosper as this system grows and prospers. It will collapse if this system collapses. But the latter is hardly likely to happen because that would be the end of world civilisation.

Indeed, the system may not collapse, but what if the system retreats, contracts or, worse, divides into two or more competing systems? We are not likely to find answers to these questions anytime soon — not least because there is "little hope of fixing the divisions in the international order," as Deputy Prime Minister Tharman Shanmugaratnam observed, till the "domestic divisions and the loss of trust in political leadership [in the advanced economies] are repaired."

Which leads me to my fourth and final observation: The divisions that DPM Tharman mentioned can occur here too, as indeed Rajaratnam foresaw 46 years ago. For in the same speech celebrating the emergence of Singapore as a global city, Rajaratnam warned:

> In this address I have dealt largely with the economic aspects of Singapore as a Global City. But the political, social and cultural implications of being a Global City are no less important.... The political, social and cultural problems, I believe, would be far more difficult to tackle. These may be the Achilles' heel of the emerging Global Cities. Laying the economic infrastructure of a Global City

may turn out to be the easiest of the many tasks involved in creating such a city. But the political, social and cultural adjustments such a city would require to enable men to live happy and useful lives in them may demand a measure of courage, imagination and intelligence which may or may not be beyond the capacity of its citizens.

We know now why the political, social and cultural adjustments attendant on becoming a global city may be more difficult than the economic adjustments. We have been grappling with these difficulties — most pronouncedly since the 2011 General Election but in reality since the 1990s. Let me end with a series of one-liner thesis statements to outline that reality:

- Singapore may be a global city, but not all parts of its economy are equally globalised;
- Singaporeans may be global citizens, but not all Singaporeans are equally cosmopolitan in their outlook;
- Communities exist here and now, locally, or they do not exist at all;
- Singapore is a global city, linked to other global cities, but there is no singular community linking these global cities;
- The global economy doubtless exists, but there is no global society subtending the global economy;
- Income inequality is ultimately due to the incomes of the globalised elite in any society outstripping the incomes of the rest in that society;
- The most privileged locally are also the most mobile globally, and the most mobile globally are also the most privileged locally;
- Meritocracy = Local Privilege = Global Mobility;
- Echoing Prime Minister Lee Hsien Loong — if we do not resolve the political, social and cultural problems attendant on Singapore being a global city, our politics will turn vicious, our society will fracture and our nation will wither.

And finally:

- We cannot secure Singapore's place in the world without first securing Singapore.

Rajaratnam's vision of Singapore as a global city is a work in progress. Let us strive, as he urged, "to make the Global City now coming into being into the Heavenly City that prophets and seers have dreamt about since time immemorial."

I

Singapore and the World

Introductory Remarks by Tommy Koh[1]

I would like to begin by thanking Janadas and the IPS family for giving me the honour of moderating this panel. It is a privilege that no money can buy. Professor Wang Gungwu is my Confucius and I am one of his many disciples. I served George Yeo three times: when he was our Minister for Information, Communication and the Arts, when he was our Minister for Trade and Industry, and when he was our Minister for Foreign Affairs. He was an inspiring and caring boss.

TOPIC OF PANEL

The topic of this panel is "Singapore and the World". I hope Janadas will not be offended when I say that I do not like the narrative for this panel scripted by IPS. The United States (US) and China are very important countries, but the world is bigger than just those two countries. For example, the biggest economy of the world is neither the US nor China; it is the European Union (EU).

THE TOP 10 DEVELOPMENTS IN 2018

In place of the IPS narrative, I offer you my list of the top 10 developments in the world in 2018.

---

[1] This text was prepared for delivery at the conference. Professor Koh's full remarks are available in video format on the IPS website.

No. 1: Singapore's place in the world

Singapore's image, brand and soft power rose to an unprecedented height in 2018. This was due to our successful hosting of the Trump-Kim Summit, our successful chairing of the Association of Southeast Asian Nations (ASEAN) and the Hollywood blockbuster *Crazy Rich Asians*.

No. 2: ASEAN's successful year

ASEAN had a very successful year. It managed to maintain its unity, neutrality and centrality. It was adroit in managing its relations with the US, China, Russia, Japan, India and the EU. For example, ASEAN conducted joint naval exercises with China in 2018 and will do the same with the US in 2019. Under the chairmanship of Singapore, ASEAN launched new initiatives in smart cities, e-commerce and cyber security.

No. 3: The TPP did not die

When President Trump pulled the US out of the Trans-Pacific Partnership (TPP), many people thought that the TPP would die. The remaining 11 members of the TPP modified it to become the Comprehensive and Progressive Agreement for Trans-Pacific Partnership (CPTPP) and it has come into force. It is open to accession by other countries, such as the United Kingdom (UK) post-Brexit. The moral of the story is that the US is important, but it is not indispensable.

No. 4: The Paris Agreement is alive and well

In a similar way, when the US announced its withdrawal from the Paris Agreement on Climate Change, some people wondered whether it would survive without the US. The happy news is that no other country has followed the US out of the agreement. Even in the case of the US, many states, cities and leading companies have pledged to honour the commitments made by the Obama Administration. The contracting parties recently held their 24th meeting in Poland. The meeting adopted the so-called Katowice Rulebook for the implementation of the Paris Agreement.

No. 5: Peace or war on the Korean Peninsula?

In 2016 and 2017, there was a danger of a nuclear war between the US and North Korea. North Korea had acquired the capacity to strike the US mainland with nuclear weapons. This was viewed by the US as an unacceptable threat to its security. In June 2018, President Trump and Chairman Kim had a historic summit in Singapore. They signed a joint communique containing four points. The officials have been unable to agree on how to implement the Singapore communique. The two leaders are planning to hold a second summit soon. The question that I wish to pose to the two panellists is: What does Chairman Kim want? Does he want to emulate Deng Xiaoping and open up North Korea, or is he dissembling?

No. 6: Free trade versus protectionism

The conventional wisdom is that free trade is a force for good. Thinkers from Adam Smith down to the present have subscribed to this view. The theory is supported by the facts. Many developing countries, especially in Asia, have been able to trade themselves out of poverty. The same is true of globalisation. There is, however, a counter-revolution, led by the US. It is to oppose free trade and globalisation, and it is championing economic nationalism and protectionism. The happy news in 2018 is that the counter-revolutionaries have not prevailed. It is therefore strategically important for us to conclude the 16-nation Regional Comprehensive Economic Partnership (RCEP) negotiations as soon as possible.

No. 7: Multilateralism at risk

The world has grown increasingly interdependent and interconnected. Trade, travel, technology and globalisation have changed forever the nature of the world we live in. Some of our most important challenges, such as global warming and climate change, the mass extinction of species, the warming and acidification of our oceans, terrorism and mass migration, can only be solved through international cooperation and multilateral institutions. In parts of the West, we have witnessed the rise of right-wing populists who emphasise nationalism and denounce so-called globalism. They wish to destroy the multilateral institutions, such as the World Trade Organization and the United Nations Educational, Scientific and Cultural

Organization (UNESCO). We must not allow these right-wing populists to prevail in this fight. At the same time, we must not allow the growing inequality in our societies to produce the phenomenon of "angry voters".

No. 8: Messy Middle East

The Middle East has never known peace in the last 70 years. The dream of a just peace between Israel and the Palestinians has vanished into the desert air. The cleavage between the Sunnis and the Shiites has deepened and become violent. This is manifested in the proxy wars in Syria and Yemen. The rivalry between Saudi Arabia and Iran has become toxic. To add to the complication, four Arab countries, namely, Bahrain, Egypt, Saudi Arabia and the United Arab Emirates, have imposed a blockade against Qatar. Incidentally, all five countries are Sunni. In the meantime, ISIS has lost most of its territory in Syria and has gone international. Its Southeast Asian franchise was responsible for the takeover of Marawi in the Philippines.

No. 9: Europe without the UK

The UK is the first country to ask to leave the EU. The departure of the UK is a loss to the EU and a loss to the UK. The two sides have not yet agreed on a divorce agreement. It is only after the divorce agreement has been approved that they will negotiate a new trade agreement, which will govern their relationship post-Brexit. The British Parliament has rejected the divorce agreement. It is unlikely that Prime Minister Theresa May will hold a second referendum. We are therefore likely to see the UK leaving the EU on 29 March 2019 without any agreement. This will have very serious repercussions for the UK, the EU and other countries, such as Singapore.

No. 10: The United States and China destined for war?

The most important development of 2018 was the paradigm change in the nature of US-China relations. The US intellectual consensus on China has changed. The Americans now believe that the era of cooperation is over and that they have entered a new era of strategic competition. The competition is not just in trade but also in technology, military power and global influence. Vice President Mike Pence's speech at the Hudson Institute on China on 4 October 2018 is a fierce attack on China. If the speech represents the Trump Administration's China policy, then we have clearly entered a new era. I do not know what the appropriate word is to describe this new era. Is it "containment", "cold war" or "*konfrontasi*"?

In preparation for this meeting, I have re-read three books: Samuel Huntington's *The Clash of Civilizations and the Remaking of World Order*, Michael Pillsbury's *The Hundred-Year Marathon* and Graham Allison's *Destined for War: Can America and China Escape Thucydides's Trap?* My questions to Gungwu and George are: First, how would they describe the new era of relations between the US and China? Second, has the rise of China instilled fear in America as the rise of Athens did in Sparta? Third, are the two countries destined for war?

Speech by
George Yeo[1]

CHINA'S DEVELOPMENT AND
THE WORLD'S RESPONSE TO IT

Two hundred years ago, from Calcutta, Raffles established Singapore as a trading post of the British East India Company for the 19th-century China trade. What we are today is profoundly shaped by that history. We are now witnessing a new China trade in the 21st century which will be much bigger than the previous one. It will take us far if we flow with it because it is for this trade that we have evolved.

In the last 40 years, China's growth has been phenomenal and impinging on the rest of the world. The Western countries, particularly the United States (US), are unsettled by the prospect of having to share global power and influence with a non-Western people. In the last year or so, there has been a sudden coalescence of anti-China sentiments in the West. The sense of economic and political rivalry is becoming more intense. When I met Graham Allison at a conference in Beijing last month, he told me that it will get much worse. The US-China trade war is only one manifestation of this rivalry.

When the per capita income of China reaches half that of the US, China's GDP will be twice that of the US. When it reaches two-thirds that of the US, China's GDP will be roughly that of the US, the EU and Japan combined.

---

[1] This text was prepared for delivery at the conference. Mr Yeo's full remarks are available in video format on the IPS website.

It is not just the fact of China's population that is important. China's population will peak at 1.44 billion in 2030, by which time India's population will be larger. What is distinctive about China is the homogeneity of its people, with over 90 per cent of Han nationality. Neither India nor Europe nor the US has the same homogeneity. For this reason, when China is united, its internal division of labour and therefore its overall productivity is awesome. But when the cycle turns, the decline is also awesome. Hence the long cycles of Chinese history.

Let me illustrate with a historical example. In 1368, Zhu Yuanzhang defeated the Mongol Yuan and reunited China. By 1405, which was a mere 37 years after the founding of Ming, Zheng He's great fleet sailed to the Western Ocean and arrived on our shores. Singapore was an important navigation point for the Ming voyages. Ma Huan's Long Ya Men (龙牙门) most probably referred to Tanjong Belayar. That Ming China, within a few decades, was able to generate the economic surplus and assemble the talent and capabilities to set sail so many ships over enormous distances shows how productive the Chinese economy is once the country is united and organised.

China's re-emergence on the global stage is therefore not without precedent. Countries in Asia have seen a re-emergent China before and are going back to their history books for lessons on how best to respond to the new China. For the US, however, the tendency is to see China in its own image, and therefore to view it as a rival who can only become more troublesome with each passing year.

US RESPONSE

So it was the way Sparta saw an emergent Athens, both Greek cities, over 2,000 years ago. The rivalry between the two city-states became a contest between two alliances, which fought over many years on land and at sea during the Peloponnesian War. Graham Allison's book on the Thucydides Trap became a best seller because of America's growing concern with the rise of China. Last October, at a conference in Poland, the former Commander of the US Army in Europe, Lieutenant General Ben Hodges, said that a war between the US and China is very likely within 15 years.

Both sides are preparing for war. They have to. But war will be madness because each has the capability to annihilate the other, and much of the world as collateral damage. However, the same can also be said of previous great wars. When popular passions are aroused, relatively minor incidents can quickly escalate. Christopher Clark wrote a famous book about how the European powers sleepwalked into the First World War. We are therefore living in dangerous times, and small countries like ours have to be very alert.

It is no exaggeration to say that the fate of the world will depend on how US-China relations are managed in coming years. Under President Trump, the US has weakened its support of international institutions like the World Trade Organization (WTO) and the United Nations, preferring to deal with other countries bilaterally. For the time being, this is advantageous to the US because of the size of its economy. However, China's economy will be bigger in the not-too-distant future, and it is not good if China were to inherit a system of bilateralised economic relationships. In fact, Imperial China perfected the system of bilateralised economic relationships through the tributary system which, in the 21st century, is good for neither China nor the US, nor the world.

Take the Trans-Pacific Partnership (TPP) as an example. It was seeded by Singapore, Brunei, New Zealand and Chile in 2005 as a way to propagate progressively a system of free trade and investment in the Asia-Pacific. Under President Obama, the US supported the TPP, but as an anti-China coalition, which was to me a mistake. But President Trump has now pulled the US out of the TPP. Without the US and China, the TPP lacks weight. I hope countries like Singapore and Japan will persuade China to join the TPP. Once China registers its interest, the US will be forced back in. If both the US and China are part of the TPP, which will then account for more than 60 per cent of global GDP, a clear way forward for the WTO will be found. We must fight against a breakdown of the international trading system which will only sharpen economic and political conflict around the world.

The TPP is particularly important for the issue of intellectual property (IP). With digitalisation, the main value of a product is in IP. A system to regulate and protect IP is vital to the health of any modern economy. While it is wrong for Western countries to deny China the right to advance technologically, it is also wrong for China to exploit weaknesses in the current WTO system to benefit itself unfairly. Increasingly, however, it is in China's own interest to support an international regime on IP. A recent survey by

Nikkei and Elsevier[2] showed China at the top of a global ranking of most-cited scientific papers in the 30 hottest technology fields. China is becoming a major producer of IP in the world. US pressure on China on IP is therefore good for China in the longer term.

Underlying the concern over the cyber security of 5G equipment is the fear that China will convert its growing technological strength to military strength. The campaign by the Five Eyes countries led by the US to block Huawei and ZTE can slow China down but will not stop its advance. Many countries will also not go along because they will be disadvantaged by denying themselves Huawei's superior technology.

NATURE OF CHINA

If China were like the US and the old Soviet Union, seeking to spread its system to other countries, then war is perhaps inevitable. But it is not in China's nature to be a missionary or a colonising power. It is too old a civilisation to nurse such ambitions. Such ventures only lead to grief in the end. Chinese leaders read and re-read Sun Zi's *The Art of War*. They know it is absolutely necessary to understand war and be prepared for it, but he is a fool who enters into war lightly; and war, once entered into, unleashes forces which are often beyond your control. The superior leader is one who achieves his objective without having to use military force, better still without the other party feeling that he has lost. Chinese statecraft avoids major surgery when there are problems, preferring instead to twiddle acupuncture points and prescribe bitter herbs. But we must expect that, as China becomes more powerful, its officials will become more assertive, especially towards smaller countries.

Being three-quarters Chinese, we in Singapore share some common cultural and philosophical characteristics with the Chinese in China. To some extent, it is easier for us to grasp China's moves and intentions. But we cannot expect the US to take such a relaxed view. In fact, we run the risk of being accused as apologists of China if we speak in China's defence. Realistically, we must expect a prolonged trial of strength between the US and China in

---

[2] See Yuki Okoshi's article on China's research and technology, which cites the report, https://asia.nikkei.com/Business/China-tech/China-s-research-papers-lead-the-world-in-cutting-edge-tech

the coming decades. This trial of strength will continue until the US political establishment is convinced that China does indeed have a different nature, with which the US can co-exist.

China has to do much more to assure the US and other countries that it is not like them. It has to be patient. Only by consistently adopting a pattern of peaceful but firm behaviour over a prolonged period and in different arenas will the Western world and others be gradually convinced. In the meantime, the oscillations between cold war and cold peace can be rough and unpleasant. Those of us who live or work in the intersection between China and the US must expect conflicting pulls as the tensions wax and wane.

Singapore exists in the intersection between China and the US. It is of vital importance that we build on our cultural closeness to China and develop a deep knowledge of the country and its leaders. The fuller our understanding of China, the greater our value to the US, China and the rest of the world. Lee Kuan Yew studied in Britain, took part in Labour Party politics and had deep links to the British establishment. Without that relationship and the support of the British establishment, he would not have been able to defeat the left in Singapore. His knowledge of the British also informed him that, if they knew of the plan for Separation in 1965, they would have stopped it, and so he kept it a secret from them. Three years after Singapore became independent, realising that it was the US that would matter the most to Singapore, he actually took time off to spend a term in Harvard, where he got to know influential Americans like Henry Kissinger. In the same way, we must now make a determined effort to broaden and deepen our knowledge of China, as what unfolds in China will have a big impact on our well-being.

At the celebration of China's 40th anniversary of reform and opening-up last December, Lee Kuan Yew was one of 10 foreign friends of China to be specially recognised. It is a high honour for Singapore and speaks of our special relationship with China. We must build on this legacy.

RE-TRIANGULATION

The rise of China has entered everyone's calculation for the future. Trump's avowedly America-first policy is accelerating the multipolar recrystallisation of the world. Every country is now re-triangulating its position vis-à-vis these two superpowers.

In our region, the pieces are all moving before our very eyes. Prime Minister Shinzo Abe's recent visit to China showed a Japan shifting while still clinging to its strategic relationship with the US. India is in the happy position of being courted by everyone and will be made use of by neither the US nor China. The US cannot stop India from buying Russia's S-400 air defence missile system. The politics of the Middle East is seeing dramatic change with the sharp fall in US dependence on Middle Eastern hydrocarbon, China's growing dependence on it, the Khashoggi affair and Trump's determination to reduce or pull out US military forces from "endless wars" in Syria and Afghanistan. Egypt, which is receiving massive Chinese support, is biding its moment. When it begins moving again, the entire Middle East will feel its weight. Down under, Australian domestic politics is torn between an old friendship with the US and the growing pull of China's economy.

In ASEAN, no country wants to have to choose between the US and China. Certainly, no one needs China as an enemy. China is already every member country's number one trading partner. The economies of ASEAN and China are becoming more integrated. Trade tension between the US and China is accelerating this process, as businesses shift production from China to Southeast Asia. When China's President Xi Jinping announced the Belt and Road Initiative in Jakarta in October 2013, he expressed the hope that bilateral trade between ASEAN and China would reach US$1 trillion by 2020. We are not likely to achieve this target, but we will not be far short of it.

For every country along the Belt and Road, the closer a country's economic relationship with China, the greater its desire to diversify because of a natural desire not to be dominated by China. Participation by the US, Japan, Europe and others is therefore welcome. The Americans, Japanese and Europeans are potential free riders, benefitting from the Belt and Road without having to pay for it. ASEAN's strategy is a simple one, which is to stay friendly to all the major powers and be absolutely neutral. However, it is a dynamic equilibrium. From time to time, we may have to lean a little to one direction or another in order to maintain overall balance.

ASEAN'S IMPORTANCE TO SINGAPORE

ASEAN's importance to Singapore cannot be overstated. A strong ASEAN provides the 10 member countries some shelter from the cold winds of superpower rivalry. It amplifies our collective influence in a wider region. It is enlightened self-interest that places ASEAN at the heart of Singapore's foreign policy.

Singapore's role in ASEAN is out of proportion to our size. This is because we are the most ASEANised country in ASEAN. If we draw a neural map of ASEAN, the densest, most connected node is Singapore. Every member country has a significant presence and stake in Singapore. As Foreign Minister, I remember the ministry having to organise the celebration of ASEAN Day every year. As ASEAN Day, on 8 August, is just one day before our National Day, we often celebrate it on 7 August instead. We never have a problem getting representatives, including schoolchildren, from all 10 member countries to participate.

Of course, we recognise that ASEAN will never be united like Europe. We are a diverse region, probably the most diverse in the world in terms of culture, language and religion. But there is a coherence in the region brought about by its position between the two great civilisational areas of China and India. We are where the monsoons bring to our shores goods, people and culture, for six months from East Asia and for six months from South and West Asia. The Malay people describe the region as *tanah di bawah angin*, the "land beneath the winds".

From time to time, conflicts break out within the region. During my time in the ASEAN chair 10 years ago, I remember Preah Vihear being of particular concern. The ethnic conflict in Rakhine State in Myanmar is a long-standing issue and of particular sensitivity to Malaysia. Recently, between Malaysia and Singapore, some old problems have resurfaced in new ways. Notwithstanding all this, we have been able to contain problems and not allow them to get out of hand. ASEAN is often criticised for its elliptical ways. But it is precisely the softness of ASEAN which takes the edge off difficult issues. The frequency of meetings among leaders, ministers and officials also puts a premium on friendship and compromise.

Indonesia, because of its size, plays an indispensable soft leadership role. It must continue to do so, because ASEAN cannot be static in the face of changes around us. Whether it is the WTO, the TPP or the South China Sea, Indonesia's leadership can make a decisive difference to ASEAN's response. When I was in government, I visited Indonesia the most and made sure that Singapore and Indonesia's positions were aligned as much as possible.

I hope that Vietnam will play a bigger role in ASEAN too. Its economy has taken off and its weight in the region is growing steadily. Vietnam is now China's biggest trading partner in ASEAN. It has a hardworking population that is obsessed with education. Vietnam has become a supplier of software programmers for Singapore-based companies.

It is not an accident that Trump's next meeting with North Korea's Kim Jong-un is likely to be held in Hanoi after the first summit in Singapore. An ASEAN venue is acceptable not only to both the US and North Korea but also to all the other members of the Six Party Talks, especially China.

RICHNESS OF SINGAPORE'S CULTURAL DNA

In discussing modern Singapore's future in the world, we have to go back to our conception 200 years ago, when Singapore quickly grew to become a major node in a global network. Modern Singapore is not intelligible in itself. There is no aspect of Singapore society which is intelligible in itself — not our genetic makeup or our culture or the languages we speak (including Singlish) or the food we enjoy or the faiths we profess. As a city-state, we only make sense against our position in Southeast Asia, larger Asia and the world.

Singapore's cultural genome is the result of its history, not just of the last 200 years since Raffles but also of the cultural genes that those who arrived on our shores brought with them from their ancestral homelands. We may be a small city-state, but our genome is huge because of this infusion from all over the world. It is the richness of our genetic inheritance and evolution which enables us to be a vital node with complex synaptic connections, not just to the region but to the world. It must be in our cultural DNA that our young become "future-proof".

Our complex and abundant cultural genome enables us to adapt to a wide range of situations. Globalisation may have peaked. Many countries may be turning inwards. Income inequality may lead to new class struggles. A new clash of civilisations may again eventuate. The future can take many different turnings. But so long as there is no cataclysm that engulfs or disperses us, we should be able to make the necessary adjustments. That indeed has been the history of Singapore, which has always been able to reinvent itself even in the face of global upheavals.

We have the innate potential to extend more synapses in the direction where they are most needed. Today we are connected to all parts of ASEAN. In the coming years, our synaptic connections to China will become denser. As India grows organically, sometimes because of government, oftentimes despite government, our connections to India will also flourish. India will inevitably become the world's second largest economy possibly by the second half of the century. With the Middle East gradually turning eastwards, our links in that direction will also grow, including our links to Israel. It is good to remember that, when Raffles founded Singapore, one of the first things he did was to persuade the Hadrami Aljunied family from Palembang to relocate here, for he knew how important a role Arab traders played in the cities of the Nusantara. With multifaceted links to ASEAN, China, India and the Middle East, there is no limit to Singapore's growth opportunities, provided we continue to cast our gaze outwards and in all directions.

We must have this sense of ourselves and of our innate capabilities. The critical element is our internal cohesion, which is really a matter of our domestic politics. Internal cohesion relies on the Singapore DNA, which evolved in response to our collective struggle for independence at the end of the Second World War. Our diversity is sometimes our weakness, but it is also our greatest strength. Singapore's multiethnic and multireligious identity cannot be based on the suppression of individual identities. Quite the opposite. We must allow separate identities to thrive, but with one critical additional requirement, which is that each must open his mind and heart to others, and to see good in them. To be Singaporean is to become bigger than who we were originally.

Last month, President Putin and President Halimah laid the foundation stone of a Russian Orthodox church in Singapore. The Russian community in Singapore is not large, no more than a few thousand. Our willingness to create space for them on our little island sends a warm message to all Russians that we have them in our heart. I met a Russian businessman who accompanied President Putin during his visit to our region. He told me that, for days afterwards, President Putin could not stop talking about the church in Singapore. A Singapore with gold onion domes shining in the bright equatorial sun changes the perception of Singapore in Russian minds and hearts. The Russians are a great people; their friendship benefits us in many ways. However, we did place one condition on the design of the church. The traditional Russian Orthodox Church's cross sits on top of a crescent, marking the Russian victory over the Muslim Golden Horde in the 14th century. Such a cross would not be appropriate in Singapore. Happily, they also have crosses which sit on top of a globe, which is what the Russian church in Singapore will have.

THE FUTURE IN US

The world is in transition to a future that is full of unknowns. The rise of China is changing the global economic and political landscape, forcing everyone to react to it. We have to watch carefully the twists and turns of US-China relations and how the rest of the world is affected and adjust our stance appropriately. There is also the leap in science and technology, which is transforming the nature of production and creating new patterns in the organisation of human society. I recommend a beautiful book written by Sydney Brenner and other scientists called *The Chronicles of Evolution*, which was published in Singapore last year. The convergence of the IT and biomedical revolutions is altering the nature of life itself and what it means to be human. We cannot anticipate the full range of challenges to mankind, but we must be alive to the changes taking place before us and around us. Our life chances are improved if we have the buffer of a united ASEAN that keeps good relations with all major powers. But the most important factor is within ourselves — our cultural DNA, our internal cohesion and our pursuit of knowledge.

Speech by Wang Gungwu[1]

SOUTHERN EURASIA

The maritime trade between the western end of the Indian Ocean and the South China Sea was led by Indians, Persians and Arabs and connected with the archipelagic peoples astride the Sunda and Malacca Straits. The Chinese responded and became one of the largest trading communities in Southeast Asia. Their activities southwards and westwards in the Nanyang led them to see the centrality of the waters around the Malay Peninsula. When the British opened Singapore to a free trade system, Chinese traders were quick to respond. Together with many others in the region, they acted as precursors to a modernising China after the 19th century.

The classic image of China is the world of the Yellow River where core ideas emerged from the plains of Hebei, Henan and Shandong and the uplands of Shanxi and Shaanxi, the cradle zones of Chinese civilisation. There was very little about the south. When that China looked south, there were at least three souths: the southeast, the southwest and the lands further south in Southeast Asia. Most of the south was peopled by what northerners called the "Hundred Yue" (Baiyue, 百越) or "Southern Man" (Nan Man, 南蠻). Those of the southwest were separately described as "Southwest Man" (Xinan Man, 西南蠻). There was no single name for peoples further south, but they included peoples from afar who came to trade at the riverine ports of Yue territory as well as the upland towns of the southwest.

---

[1] This text was prepared for delivery at the conference. Professor Wang's full remarks are available in video format on the IPS website.

The Qin and Han rulers conquered the lands of the Baiyue. These lands later attracted large numbers of settlers from the north. The authorities left most of the Xinan Man alone. The most important changes came during the fourth century when invasions by the ancestors of peoples later known as Turkic, Tibetan and Mongol brought Han China to an end. Through collaborations between these invaders and Han people, they established a series of northern dynasties. The Han who refused to accept that moved south across the Yangzi.

There was thus a new "China" under a succession of four Southern kingdoms. But it was the Sinicised descendants of the northern dynasties that brought "south China" back into the fold. By the Tang dynasty, the economy of the Yangzi delta region was highly developed, and the empire's growth centres had shifted southwards. With growing wealth and cultural confidence, these *Tangren* in the south could say that they were more Chinese.

Another period of division followed when Khitan, Tangut, Jurchen and Mongol forces in succession pressed the Han Chinese of the Song to move its capital south of the Yangzi. There, the southerners concentrated on building the Song kingdom and redefined the idea of *tianxia* by reinterpreting the Confucian classics and drawing on the wisdom of Buddhist and Daoist thinkers and practitioners. With this revived Confucianism, they claimed to have saved the core values of civilisation. This was achieved because the enterprising southerners developed the economic potential of the coasts and combined that with the cultural authority of those who had come south over the centuries. The separation enabled the south to gain its own authoritative voice and gave its literati the right to shape the future China. But the Song Chinese failed to put a broken China back together again. When Kublai Khan conquered the kingdom, China was again unified but, this time, it was northern *non*-Chinese who ruled *all* of China.

This reintegration of China's south was a total success. The Mongols also incorporated the lands of the "Southwest Man", notably the Dali kingdom bordering Vietnam, Laos and Myanmar. Thereafter, the Ming and Qing empires steadily dismantled the autonomous chieftainships of that region. Today, officials appointed by Beijing control the towns and prefectures where minority peoples may hold key administrative positions. The last two dynasties kept China united while the Qing emperors pushed north and west to create a larger empire across Eurasia and redraw the map of China.

CHINA'S SOUTH

The elite families who moved to the south retained as much as they could of the cultural traits that their ancestors had brought with them. But over time, these *Tangren* adapted to living in terrains quite different from those in the north. Most of them settled in the valleys of smaller rivers that flowed into the East China and South China seas. These were separated by high hills and evolved into different kinds of communities. Those at the river mouths developed trading centres, some large enough for them to establish local kingdoms during periods of division. These included the Qiantang River of the Wu Yue kingdom in the 10th century and later the Southern Song; the Min River and the kingdom of Min of Fujian; and rivers like Jiulong and Han, where Hokkien and Teochiu speakers established ports and shipping centres that produced some of the most adventurous traders of the China seas. Beyond that, the Pearl River delta produced the famous kingdom of Nan Yue with its capital in Guangzhou. And then another riverine state, Lo Yue, kingdom of the Red River, whose chiefs were later able to establish the independent kingdom of Dai Viet (now Vietnam).

These southern kingdoms became sites for riverine states, but they could never combine their power to reunify all of China. It is interesting to see that large parts of southern China developed under riverine conditions similar to those of the mainland parts of Southeast Asia, where port cities also became the capitals of strong states. The best examples were the port towns along the coast of central Vietnam, where small rivers flowed into the South China Sea. The trading centres functioned as a distinct polity known as Linyi and later as Champa. Similarly, the maritime polity of Funan became part of the Khmer state of the great Mekong River that grew to become the Angkor empire. And, further west, there arose along the Menam River the Siamese state that was strong but never secure against enemies from their west. There, the delta areas of the Salween and Irrawaddy rivers protected the interior, where the upland Burma established their kingdoms.

Foreign traders coming to China were always welcome, but Chinese merchants went south in their own ships only after the 10th century. The Mongol invasion unleashed China's outreach by using the Song navies to look for more places to conquer, and attacked Japan, Vietnam, Champa and Java. Kublai Khan did all that 120 years before Zheng He. By the time the

Chinese became one of the largest groups trading between China and the Indian Ocean, the Ming dynasty decided to integrate all foreign trade in a tributary system to control all foreign trade. However, the entrepreneurs of Guangdong and Fujian continued to trade privately whenever they could.

The southern elites tended to look north to the power centre in Beijing, while their merchant compatriots saw their well-being linked to the South China Sea ports. The merchants took great risks in their enterprise, but their potential for China's economic development was rarely appreciated. The consequences of this neglect became obvious in the 19th century. Even after two Opium Wars, the literati were confident that the southern borders were manageable and could not see that radical changes further south and west had become an existential threat to their civilisation.

In the 20th century, the traditional elites were replaced by a generation who looked to the West for enlightenment, notably in the sciences and commercial and industrial enterprises. Seeking modernisation, they wanted to learn everything they could to make China strong and prosperous again. The new national consciousness also sought to revive a sense of pride in past Chinese achievements, something like the "China dream" that leaders from Sun Yat-sen down to Xi Jinping were to share. At the dream's core was the integration of the Chinese nation as *Zhonghua minzu*, backed by enterprising southerners who mastered new methods to take advantage of economic opportunities. However, young idealists objected to anything linked to foreign capitalists and sided with the Chinese Communist Party (CCP). That new China led by Mao Zedong adopted revolutionary goals that reversed the earlier modernisation efforts and returned to some traditional positions whereby political and military elites allowed the southerners only peripheral roles in the country's development.

Deng Xiaoping's decision to open up the economy to the outside world was a game-changer. By recognising how much the market economy depended on an open maritime outlook, he enabled China to develop at astonishing speed since the 1980s. This was a great leap forward for China's entrepreneurs, who played a vital role in that transformation. In addition, it also led the CCP leaders to proclaim that they needed naval power to protect their widespread economic interests. Although power is still centralised in Beijing, the openness that southerners have always wanted has stimulated high levels of dynamism in the economy. The country now understands the need to defend China's maritime interests but needs to do more to unleash the energies of its venturesome southerners.

THE REGION'S NEW FUTURE

The changing conditions further south, whether at sea or on land, clearly require China's close attention. The post-war Anglo-American powers saw Southeast Asia as potentially the centre of a new strategic zone. This region has an extraordinary history. From a number of trading kingdoms and autonomous port cities, they became territories dominated by the West. But their peoples kept faith with their community interests and drew lessons from that period of subordination. Today, they are building nation-states with distinct identities, and their leaders are keener than ever to protect their countries' sovereignty. Although this task exposes a variety of tensions within and without, the leaders have come together as members of a regional association to safeguard their interests against big power rivalries.

The region has always been diverse and had regularly fragmented into small polities for whom working together was not normal. The Vietnam War divided it into two parts. But fear of the domino effect of a communist victory pushed Thailand and four maritime states to form the Association of Southeast Asian Nations (ASEAN). After that war, ASEAN's intervention in Cambodia placed it on the side of China and made a friendly relationship possible. By the 1990s, all 10 states of Southeast Asia had set aside their differences to make the organisation fully representative of the region.

China has engaged the global market economy and connected vigorously with Western Europe and the United States (US). Its leaders moved quickly to propose an ASEAN-China Free Trade Area and supported other initiatives to bring ASEAN's commercial interests closer. This brought the South China Sea, which China shares with eight of the Southeast Asian nations, to the centre of that relationship. When China became the world's second-largest economy and showed its determination to control its maritime claims, their island-building activities led the US to highlight freedom of navigation for its naval forces. Together with the ideological differences between the two powers, China's claims are now presented as threats to the security of several ASEAN nations.

China's south is more open than ever, but Beijing leaders remain in strict control and have discovered new ways to move forward. This has led to one of the country's biggest ideas, the "One Belt One Road" initiative that seeks to create more opportunities for future economic growth. Its key feature is that it covers both the overland and maritime potentials across the whole stretch of the Old Eurasian World, where a balanced approach is essential to advance China's long-term interests.

The overland Silk Road and the growing dependence on access to maritime ports are two sides of the vision whereby China safeguards its national goals in both directions at the same time. Nevertheless, the distinction between the overland belt and the maritime road is important, and the Chinese expect that the challenges facing each half would be different. The overland belt across Eurasia to reach markets in Europe has not been attractive for centuries. What distinguishes China's new approach is that this belt also reaches southwards to the Indian Ocean. Here, geopolitical advantage is more important, and that has induced neighbouring states to join the organisation.

China's south, the maritime "Silk Road", is a different story. It is now central to future economic development, and keeping the waters secure for China's maritime linkages has never been so vital. For the first time in history, the south is an existential problem for its national interests. There are at least three dimensions to the changing conditions.

Firstly, the dynamism in globalisation depends a great deal on entrepreneurs and inventive industrialists, who are always more active and better appreciated in China's south. Chinese northern leaders claim to understand the need to give them fuller rein to devise the best methods for the Belt and Road Initiative (BRI) to grow, but are still too prone to impose tight controls at the slightest provocation.

Secondly, the countries to China's south are now sovereign states in an overarching international system and have organised themselves to protect the region. This is not to say that ASEAN is united — it is obvious that its members are still seeking unity in several key areas. But the association has come a long way, and its members understand how important it is for them to do things together. China's leaders would need to do everything they can to help them stay together and not allow outside forces to create dangerous and unnecessary divisions.

Thirdly, the South China Sea has become a source of tension between the United States and China. The subject now involves countries not bordering the sea, including US allies like Japan and Australia, and some countries of the European Union. As a focal point in the US reaction to China's rise, ASEAN members know that it is more crucial than ever to be united. When the Americans redefined their strategic concerns by moving the goalposts from the Asia-Pacific to the Indo-Pacific, the decision made Southeast Asia more central to the competing powers. No one is certain how the threats to peace and prosperity can be eliminated. Mere regular meetings between ASEAN and its partner states may not be enough if either China or the US insists that ASEAN has to decide which side it supports.

China's entrepreneurial classes have to face these factors confronting the Silk Road in China's south. They know the region and are unlikely to take the unity of ASEAN for granted. They also have to ensure that their northern leaders understand the demands of coastal and maritime outreach as well as the different demands of the economies across ASEAN's land borders. The proposals to connect China's southwestern provinces to the South China Sea and the Bay of Bengal through Vietnam, Laos, Thailand and Myanmar point to the importance of the land-sea dimensions of the BRI and the measures needed to ensure that both parts of the initiative support each other.

Furthermore, there are now millions of settlers of Chinese descent in Southeast Asia who are loyal to their respective nation-states. Most people in southern China are able to relate to these communities and know how to deal with them with care. But those responsible among the central elites, especially those of northern origins, have not found these localised communities easy to understand. If China hopes that these nationals of Chinese descent would play a positive role in their countries' relations with China, it would have to exercise sensitivity to their local interests as well as the interests of the countries where they have made their homes.

ASEAN is now being re-envisaged as a strategic zone for all the powers. This is because the economic dynamism centred in the North Atlantic for the past two centuries is moving to the southeast regions of the Old World. More recently, the shift from Europe to the Indian Ocean underlines how timely the BRI is and why it is taking advantage of this development to highlight its long-term benefits to a revived Old World.

Such a move will not be as straightforward as the US reacting by redefining their new strategic interest in the Indo-Pacific. For those in the Old World, the Western Pacific and Indian Oceans have always been where all kinds of Eurasian protagonists traded for millennia, where the exchange of ideas, cultures and goods has been conducted under conditions of relative peace. Those historical relationships show how that Old World has been interconnected. A fresh review of that history would help the peoples involved to restore the conditions that ensured that every part of that larger trading zone benefitted from the trading relations.

The Indo-Pacific as redefined by a hegemonic power on the other side of the Pacific means that Southeast Asia, as the only region that faces both oceans, will become more critical than ever. Singapore, once part of the commercial zone that connected the two halves of the Old Eurasian World, has been transformed into a global node in the Anglo-American order. Given that its location is also central to China's future in the south, the city-state would need to find new ways to perform its dual roles, one in a revived Eurasia and the other in a globalised world. It will not be doing this alone. But it will have to devote much of its energies to ensure that fellow members of ASEAN all understand the region's role and work together to avoid being destroyed by big power rivalries.

II

Singapore and International Economics

Introductory Remarks
by Gabriel Lim[1]

I am looking forward to a very good discussion because I have two excellent speakers with me.

My fellow speakers, Chee Koon and Kai Fong, and I are pretty much of the same vintage — the post-65 generation. We attended university in the early 1990s, which I think we would all agree was quite an unusual and different time. It was a few years after the Cold War. It was also very soon after the "Washington Consensus" was set out, and the subsequent 20 to 25 years (since the early 1990s) have been a period of remarkable growth and prosperity for the world. Various estimates peg global growth at about 3.5 times over the last 25 years. Singapore has grown, maybe, eight to 10 times. It is quite a remarkable story, and the three of us here are fortunate to have been a part of that trajectory. Of course, there were blips. There were very difficult recessions, like the Asian Financial Crisis; we were confronted with Severe Acute Respiratory Syndrome; and there was the global financial crisis about 10 years ago. But, overall, I think it is fair and accurate to say that it has been a time of sustained prosperity, peace and general growth all round, but especially in Singapore.

However, it almost seems as if the wheels are sort of coming off or are certainly getting a bit loose. Deputy Prime Minister Tharman Shanmugaratnam at Davos had spoken about dark clouds over the horizon. True as it may be, nevertheless, I have with me on this panel two of the more optimistic and most forward-looking people I know in my generation, whose job it is to look for that silver lining in these dark clouds, to look for that pot

---

[1] This edited transcript was prepared by the Institute of Policy Studies (IPS). Mr Lim's full remarks are available in video format on the IPS website.

of gold at the end of the rainbow, and actually find a way to take full advantage of that, to take Singapore and their organisations forward.

Now, the gentleman on my left, Lee Chee Koon. First of all, congratulations on not just being promoted to the role of Group CEO of CapitaLand Limited but — with the Ascendas-Singbridge deal in the works — the possibility of leading what will be the ninth largest real estate company in Asia, with over a hundred billion dollars in assets. To say that your rise up the corporate ladder has been meteoric is a bit of an "insult" to meteors. But all I can say is, it is fully well deserved. I have known Chee Koon for over 30 years, so I have the luxury of poking fun at him. He started off as a civil servant, left civil service, I think, 12 to 13 years ago, but in the short space of time while there, he oversaw the organisation of the 2006 International Monetary Fund World Bank Group Ministers Meetings right down the road at Suntec — a massive enterprise. He had also worked with Mr George Yeo on quite a few free trade agreements. And now, Chee Koon is right at the cusp of building up CapitaLand and flying the flag for Singapore in global markets.

On my right is Chng Kai Fong. He is the Managing Director of the Economic Development Board (EDB), responsible for attracting tens of billions of dollars of investments into Singapore. He was, until recently, the Principal Private Secretary to Prime Minister Lee Hsien Loong. He is someone who is widely known to be independent, creative and unconventional. He is one of the sharpest, most creative and brilliant minds in the civil service, and certainly at the vanguard of the next generation of civil servants. Kai Fong has been a career civil servant, but he did spend a couple of years in Shell. His responsibilities in EDB now includes strengthening Singapore's position as a global city, attracting foreign investments into Singapore, creating new jobs for our future generations, and essentially making sure that we have many, many more years of success, growth and prosperity. With this, I would like to turn the microphone over to Kai Fong.

SESSION

Speech by
Chng Kai Fong[1]

DAVOS DIVIDE

Most of you would have read about dark clouds surrounding the global economy: United States (US)-China strategic competition; China's economy; workers being disrupted by globalisation and technology. I do not think I can add to the analysis out there.

One encounter in Davos stands out. At a breakfast hosted by a large European bank, the chief executive officer (CEO) started by taking a vote: "Who thinks globalisation and technology are good things for society?" Eighty-five per cent of the audience voted yes. Thereafter, speaker after speaker spoke optimistically about the world, for example, on the potential of artificial intelligence (AI) to transform lives.

Then, a prime minister of a small country spoke. He said, "Here, we in Davos overwhelmingly support free trade and technology, because we feel the benefits. But back home, my voters do not. If you ask them the same question, more than half will say no."

How refreshing for a politician to be so frank.

Deputy Prime Minister Tharman Shanmugaratnam wrote the same in his Facebook post:

---

[1] This text was prepared for delivery at the conference. This version has been edited by IPS for the purpose of inclusion in this publication. The full speech by Mr Chng is available in video format on the IPS website.

39

But the biggest difficulties lie within nations themselves. People are now deeply divided in the advanced nations that led the world for decades (Japan is an exception).

Until these domestic divisions and the loss of trust in political leaders [are] repaired, there is little hope of fixing the divisions in the international order. A spirit of common interests globally, and of wanting to resolve problems in a cooperative way, will not return until there is a sense of shared interests among people at home, in their own societies....

Politicians of all stripes, and businesses too, need the humility to understand why ordinary working people have voted this way. There was more humility in Davos this year than in the past.

That encapsulates the dilemma that all countries, big and small, are facing today, including Singapore.

CHANGE, CONSTANCY AND COURAGE

Why the divide? It is because the old paradigm has changed. The liberal world order of free trade and open markets is being pulled back. In business, the internet and digitalisation of operations has led to upheavals. For example, Economic Development Board (EDB) used to chase manufacturers to invest because when "one controls supply, one controls demand". Ford used to say, "You can have a car in any colour, so long as it is in black." It shows the power of the supplier. But with digitalisation, the tables have turned. Now, if one controls the demand first, one controls the supply. We see this with Uber, Facebook and Netflix. For workers, it used to be working for one company the whole of your life, after studies. Now, you have to be prepared to constantly learn to upgrade, to change jobs, and to be adaptable.

Janadas Devan, the Director of IPS, started today by referencing Rajaratnam's "Global City" speech in 1972. It was remarkably prescient, and the vision, remarkably enduring. The early years leading up to 1972 were tumultuous, and the paradigm was upended. In 1959, Singapore was dealing with self-government, having freed ourselves from British rule, and we had to deal with the Communist United Front. In 1963, we merged with Malaysia, hoping to sell to the common market, but racial riots and tensions reared their heads, and in 1965, we became independent. In 1968, the British announced their withdrawal from Singapore, resulting in a drop of 20 per cent in the gross domestic product (GDP) of Singapore.

Yet, guided by the Global City vision and our leaders, by 1972, we had overcome our challenges, and grew 10 to 12 per cent on average. Foreign investments poured in. We created many jobs, trained our people for them. Unemployment declined rapidly, and living standards rose, such that in one generation, we leapfrogged from Third World to First. The best essay on how we achieved this was written by our economic architect himself, Dr Goh Keng Swee. "A socialist economy that works" described Singapore's unique economic model — blending together laissez-faire economics, and state intervention, with a practical, results-oriented bent.

To refer to past speeches to find the success formula today would be foolhardy. But what must remain constant is our cast of mind, the same which our leaders in the past displayed. They were humble, always seeking to learn from the best. They saw the world for what it was, not what it should have been. They bravely stood for what they believed in and were determined to pull everyone together and point towards the vision. In the words of Dr Goh:

> Singapore's political leaders had often to assume the role of Moses when he led the children of Israel through the wilderness in search of the Promised Land. We had to exhort the faithful, encourage the faint-hearted and censure the ungodly.

It was this cast of mind that saw us through difficult periods in the last 50 years, and enabled us to go against conventional wisdom and succeed. For example, in the 1960s, when everyone was preaching import substitution for developing countries, we took Dr Albert Winsemius' advice and chased export-oriented industries. A few years after we achieved self-government from the British and freed ourselves from colonialism, we chased multinational corporations (MNCs) to invest in Singapore to build our capabilities and train our workers. In 1984, when we encountered our first recession, we started from a blank sheet: We reduced our labour costs, improved our labour market's flexibility, liberalised the information and communications technology and finance sectors, and created a second engine

41

of growth. In all circumstances, we were unafraid to swallow bitter medicine, and the results proved us right.

CAUTIOUSLY CONFIDENT

It is this cast of mind that we in this generation must seek to emulate. We are now at a turning point again. Dark clouds are hovering. What can Singapore do?

I am cautiously confident for three reasons.

One, we are differentiated. We are differentiated from the world. While others are in slower regions, Singapore is in the heart of ASEAN, which will be among the fastest growing regions in the world. The world is waking up to ASEAN. At Davos, the Indonesian night was packed to standing room only, and it was not just because of the food.

We are also differentiated within ASEAN. Singapore can play a role because we are urban and well connected, a place where talent wants to come. Our workforce is talented, and we have a strong reputation for trust. That is why many companies situate their regional headquarters in Singapore, even while they have substantial operations in other ASEAN countries.

Two, we have a head start in transforming ourselves. At Davos, one of the hot topics was the impact of AI and automation on workers. Just last week, Brookings Institution released a sobering report, which concluded that small US cities, rural communities and Rust Belt states were most at risk. The prescription of the report was to embrace growth and technology, promote a constant learning mindset, facilitate smoother adjustment, reduce hardships for workers who are struggling, and mitigate harsh local impacts.

These prescriptions are remarkably similar to DPM Tharman's Economic Review Committee and Minister Heng's Committee on the Future Economy (CFE) reports. That is why, today, we have SkillsFuture Singapore and Workforce Singapore, institutions that have workers at the heart of their mission. With the Industry Transformation Maps, our businesses and unions have been transforming themselves. We identified the problem almost eight years ago and have been working on them. That is why Klaus Schwab, the founder of the World Economic Forum (WEF), suggested to WEF participants: "Look at Singapore. They are doing all these to prepare their people." I do not think we have cracked the code, but we have a head start and the wherewithal to make the change.

Three, and most importantly, we are holding together as a society. Contrast that to the news around the world, on Brexit, on politics drifting to the extremes. The world is rife with countries that are internally divided. To businesses, the premium for stability and trust has increased significantly. There will be an even greater premium because with technology, capital and talent are becoming more important. Being small now gives us an advantage, because we are nimble, and we can effectively implement structures and systems that will hold us together — whether it is strengthening our safety nets, workfare, investing in education or building our communities in our Housing & Development Board (HDB) towns.

SINGAPORE'S STRATEGY

But we have a lot more work ahead. Others can easily catch up and we will soon lose our head start. Take, for example, financial payments and e-commerce. In just eight years, China has leapfrogged with Alibaba and WeChat. Indonesia startups are scaling up at blistering speeds. Malaysia released a strategy for advanced manufacturing, which is broadly similar to ours. The United Kingdom (UK) government's industrial strategy white paper talks about "sector deals", which bring businesses, workers and government together, somewhat similar to our Industry Transformation Maps. I mentioned it to my UK counterpart, and he said he had studied our CFE report. Other countries have far smarter people and can come up with far more comprehensive plans than we can. The difference is never about the plans. It is execution.

So, let me share five priority areas of our economic strategy that we want to execute.

First, ASEAN. We have to get more plugged in, not just physically but culturally. As a people, we must know ASEAN better because that is how we are going to make our living, by facilitating the connections with ASEAN and the world. Our young people do not know ASEAN well. On a business trip to Kuala Lumpur, I was shocked to find out that one of my young colleagues had not been to Malaysia before! Our universities have many overseas immersion programmes, but the first choice of many students is always the US or Europe. ASEAN hardly ranks among their choices. Ngee Ann Polytechnic has a good programme where they send students to intern at companies in ASEAN. EDB works with ASEAN companies to take in

Singaporean graduates as interns. These students come back changed, because their eyes are opened to the opportunities in ASEAN. We have to do more, because that is how we will make our living, by connecting the world to ASEAN.

Second, digital. Digital plays to our strengths, because we are highly connected and our workers are skilled. Digitalisation has caused upheaval to many industries, rendering some industries obsolete and rendering what was previously unviable industries viable. For example, it is now possible to manufacture cars and build an ecosystem for autonomous vehicles in Singapore. Previously, agriculture required a lot of land. Now, with the use of AI and sensors, and drawing from the example of the Netherlands, intensive farming is possible in Singapore. We need to help our companies to take advantage of the digital revolution, to be able to sell their products and services overseas.

Third, innovation. Our economy must shift from a knowledge-driven to an innovation-led one. To capture the most value, we have to create new products, new services out of Singapore. That will be through design, through engineering and through understanding customers better.

Fourth, linkages. We need a thick economy and strong clusters comprising MNCs, small and medium enterprises (SMEs) and startups. In 1972, Dr Goh explained our industrial policy in an essay:

> We want our industries to be so structured that components strengthen each other, and we maximise our gains from external economies of scale.... [from] supply of components ... [to] a more effective training programme... it will be easier to mount a research and development effort... [Then in the long term], Singaporeans will not only be able to man the technical management positions, but also to contribute to product development and innovation.

Dr Goh went on to observe that it will not be useful if we have one petrochemical plant here, one watch factory there. All disparate, serving their global HQs. They have to be linked.

Strong linkages are not just about the supply chain or R&D but also talent. MNCs provide good training grounds for workers to learn how to build organisational capabilities and manage complex systems. If there is a healthy circulation of workers between MNCs, SMEs and startups, it would give our economy a boost and we will have a better chance of transforming our SMEs into MNCs and giants.

Fifth, inclusion. To make all these things work, we must continue to hold together. Inclusion must be a foremost consideration in our economic strategy. We cannot just deal with inclusion ex-post, but it has to be factored in ex-ante in our policy formulation. For example, it is not just the number of jobs that EDB brings in, but we also need to consider the type of jobs we bring in and how it can help inclusion.

A young person asked, by what measures will we know if we have succeeded in 30 years? I replied, apart from GDP, which will still be important, we have to measure gross national income, which gives an indication of whether we succeeded in creating opportunities for our Singaporeans in ASEAN and the rest of the world. We also have to measure inclusion and inequality. Finally, we have to measure innovation, through metrics of intellectual property, R&D spending and number of startups.

CONCLUSION

So, what is my answer to whether globalisation and technology have been good for society?

I know of a single mother that runs a cleaning business for offices. She cannot speak English, but she has a network of office ladies whom she can assign to clean offices. The business was earning about $100,000 a year — not big, but she could make do. She has one son whom she put through school and who, got a scholarship and went to Stanford to study Computer Science.

In Stanford, he discovered search engine optimisation (SEO) and decided to optimise search rankings for his mother's business. Before long, his mother's business grew to $2 million a year. He wanted to test the potential overseas. So, he did SEO in that country and got a phone line in that country to gauge the response. The business rose to number one in the search rankings, and the phone line was flooded with calls, even though there were technically no operations in that country.

So, globalisation and technology have the potential to be good for society. They have democratised tools and expanded markets, such that anyone can start and grow a business successfully.

But is it truly good? The tale of the mother and the son is also a cautionary tale. Imagine that the son did not go to Stanford. Then the business could have languished. It illustrates the divide between the haves and the have-nots. There is a tremendously exciting world out there, full of opportunities, but you need the knowledge and the skills to exploit it.

How do we bring the world of the cleaning mother and the world of the Stanford son together more intentionally and deliberately? Part of it must be through education, so that each generation has many more opportunities and access. But it is not enough. There must be active intervention on all our parts — governments, businesses and unions — to pull people together, to share knowledge, to create opportunities for each other.

So, I replied that, yes, I am optimistic about the potential of globalisation and technology, but I am pessimistic about whether we can bridge the divide.

But, in Singapore, we must and can buck the trend.

II

Speech by
Lee Chee Koon[1]

I would like to share my perspectives at three different levels: country, company and individual.

COUNTRY

At the country level, Singapore is quite widely known as a little red dot, a small country of five million. No hinterland, no natural resources. But it has beaten the odds to not only survive but thrive. In my view, it has certainly punched above its weight. As a country, we are known to be among the most competitive, least corrupt and safest. Our airports and ports are also internationally renowned. Many countries are trying to learn from our governance structure, how we are managing our reserves, and even as basic as learning from our education system, our Housing & Development Board (HDB), and so on. We are also seen as a neutral country. That is why we got to play host for the Trump-Kim Summit and earlier meetings between Taiwan and China.

I am starting my remarks with some positivity, because it sometimes feels unfashionable to speak well of Singapore these days. But truth be told, we are the envy of many countries, and I have met many people and friends who would hope to become Singapore permanent residents or Singaporeans. These include very rich, very successful people, who want to call Singapore home. While I understand fellow Singaporeans do have some grouses (Mass Rapid Transit (MRT) breakdowns, cost of living, etc.), I think we should not

---

[1] This text was prepared for delivery at the conference. This version has been edited by IPS for the purpose of inclusion in this publication. The full speech by Mr Lee is available in video format on the IPS website.

always see the glass as half empty. We have not done too badly. We are not quite where we want to be, but we are in a better position than most.

We are a small country. We must be realistic of the influence we can exert, but our ambition must never be limited by our physical size. We need to continue to evolve, innovate and stay relevant as an important node in the global system, so that we can continue to attract talent, capital, new investments and ideas to our country, to position our country and our economy for the future. I was very happy to see the recent announcements by Dyson to move its electric car manufacturing facilities and its corporate headquarters to Singapore.

In fact, in a world where we see a gradual breakdown of the international world order, where there are trade disputes, government shutdowns and the fight for technological supremacy, there might be a niche where Singapore can make ourselves even more relevant — in a world where countries, companies and individuals are seeking stability, protection and trust.

COMPANY

At the company level, the reality is that Singapore's domestic market is too small. So, for any company that wants to become a significant player, it needs to first go regional and then, if it makes sense, go global. When CapitaLand was first formed in early 2000, the focus was to go regional. We made bold moves and today, we have built up a vertically integrated business in China, Vietnam and Malaysia. More recently, CapitaLand has announced a transaction to combine with Ascendas-Singbridge. The ambition here is really to build a global real estate company that is diversified across different asset classes. So, first regionalisation before globalisation.

While it is enchanting to shout globalisation, execution is far from easy. There are issues relating to market access, dealing with local governments, brand awareness, taxes, joint venture partners, recruiting and sending talent, and the list goes on. Every different operating geography brings a different set of challenges. But we have no choice, because our domestic market is limited.

And once you have made the decision to establish your presence somewhere, you cannot run away at the first sign of trouble. I recall, in my second month of posting to Shanghai, there was a group of men with crew-cut hairstyle waiting below my office. They had been sent by contractors who wanted us to agree to the changes to the contract sum arising from variation orders. My family was staying in one of the apartments above the office. These are issues that we have to deal with. And then, during the March 2011 earthquake in Fukushima, there was widespread fear of nuclear radiation. Some foreign companies actually shut down their operations and extricated their staff. But Ascott stayed on. Because our colleagues were there. Because our customers were there. It was our corporate responsibility. And I recall having this conversation with my wife, that I had to go and visit my team to give them moral support. We had only had our first kid then, and my wife was concerned about possible radiation exposure to me. But I had no choice. It was a leadership responsibility.

Globalisation is even more difficult when we have to start building our base out of Singapore. Using the hospitality business as an example, when you look at Marriott, InterContinental Hotels Group and Accor, these companies have been around for decades, and many of them were able to build a solid base of business in their sizeable domestic markets before venturing overseas. When I was running Ascott, we had to compete with these big boys. Today, Ascott has about 100,000 keys worldwide, which sounds like a lot but is a far cry from the biggest player, Marriott, having more than 1.3 million. Even though Ascott opens something like 40 properties a year, or three a month, this is nothing compared to the bigger players, like my good friends in China, Huazhu, which opens about three hotels a day. So, this is the order of things and the competition that we are dealing with, not to mention tech disruptors like Airbnb and others.

Despite all these challenges, to me, globalisation is par for the course if we truly want to become a significant player. But every company will need to define its own niche, be clear of its own advantages and capabilities, and be determined about getting to the end point.

One interesting observation made by many people is that Singapore companies are not good at working together in overseas markets, unlike the Koreans, Japanese, Taiwanese or even the Chinese. Instead, they tend to compete with each other. It is a familiar sight to see "cousin" companies bidding for the same projects as CapitaLand abroad. My view is that, if we can get more Singapore companies to work together (assuming every company can deliver at the right level) in seeking opportunities in overseas markets, over time, we should see greater success among Singapore companies in overseas markets.

It is important for Singapore to build up a number of strong global enterprises beyond just Creative, BreadTalk, Charles and Keith, and the stable of Temasek-linked companies. I am sure we can do much better than this, to help extend the economic space for Singapore and also to create job opportunities for Singaporeans, which brings me to my final point.

INDIVIDUAL

At the individual level, how do we make Singaporeans globally aware, globally connected and globally competitive?

Competition for jobs is intensifying. There are many people who can and want to do our jobs. If you look around the world, there are millions of people who are young and qualified, yet unemployed. Many of these people are packing up and leaving their home countries, armed with master's degrees and PhDs, and moderate salary expectations. They are prepared to go to China, learn Mandarin and immerse in the culture, and compete for jobs that pay non-expat packages.

By comparison, it is relatively more difficult to get Singaporeans to take up overseas assignments, unless these are in Shanghai, Tokyo, Sydney, New York, London and the usual suspect cities. Even so, some would demand to return to Singapore to settle down or put their kids through the Singapore education system. Many also expect to be paid expat packages, even those who are on overseas training.

I was recently told by a CEO of a large regional company that they have given up hiring Singaporeans for their management trainee programme. They would instead choose people from Malaysia, because they are more affordable to recruit, less demanding and more prepared to take on "hardship assignments".

There is no way we can teach hunger. But what we can do is to encourage Singaporeans to keep a competitive mindset, to be prepared to venture out of their comfort zone, to take the road less travelled, to learn to manage uncertainty. We are seeing some early results, with more Singaporeans in the startup scene. Not all the startups will succeed, but the experiences and lessons one would have picked up in starting up new enterprises would be highly invaluable and would certainly better prepare one for a future that will be fraught with disruptions.

We have to accept that the shelf life of paper qualifications will be limited. We will be expected to change jobs and industries and pick up new skills in the course of our work life. We must continue to grow and evolve; build up skills, networks and global perspectives that will allow us to take the very top jobs. How much we want to learn, how much we want to value add, how much we want to achieve is very much up to us.

III

Singapore and the Region

SESSION

Introductory Remarks
by Chan Heng Chee[1]

I feel very privileged to be chairing this session today on Singapore and the region, because both of our speakers are the leading strategic thinkers of the region. I have with me Dr Marty Natalegawa, former Foreign Minister of Indonesia, from the years 2009 to 2014 in the government of President Susilo Bambang Yudhoyono. Now, Pak Marty is a career diplomat. He was Ambassador to the United Kingdom and then Indonesia's Permanent Representative to the United Nations, where he served until 2009 and returned home to be Foreign Minister. But since leaving his position, he has been appointed to the United Nations Secretary-General's High-Level Advisory Board on Mediation. Now what is important is that, recently, Dr Marty published a book titled *Does ASEAN Matter? A View from Within.*

Now, I have here on my right, Mr Bilahari Kausikan, whom you all know as a career diplomat. He served as Ambassador to the Russian Federation and then as Singapore's Permanent Representative to the United Nations. He had been with the foreign ministry for a long time, where he became Permanent Secretary for Foreign Affairs. He was my boss. He was also my student — I taught him in the university. Bilahari became Ambassador-at-Large after he stepped down as Permanent Secretary. He has since finished his stint as Ambassador-at-Large and is now Chairman of the Middle East Institute at the National University of Singapore. Bilahari's most recent book is titled *Singapore Is Not An Island: Views on Singapore Foreign Policy.*

Both these writer-diplomats, given what they have written, are really well equipped to discuss and speak on Singapore and the region, and what is

---

[1] This edited transcript was prepared by the Institute of Policy Studies (IPS). Professor Chan's full remarks are available in video format on the IPS website.

happening in the region. This morning, we had a robust discussion in the first session, "Singapore and the world", and then we had a very interesting discussion on "Singapore and international economics". I think some of the themes of Singapore and the world will be reflected in this session.

We all know that Southeast Asia is the theatre of great-power rivalry. It is where the big economic ideas, economic trends and social trends are sweeping over and reshaping our world. It is an area where a lot of things are happening. What sense do we make of what is happening? In a sense, this is an area that will see disruption. It will not be business as usual, but the disruption does not only come from external forces such as the United States, China and globalisation. It is also coming from within the region, because Southeast Asia is a region with heterogeneous societies and great diversity. It is a region where race and religion are always salient sources of conflict, be it Myanmar, Malaysia, Indonesia, Philippines, Singapore or Vietnam. It is a place of rising nationalisms. It is also a place of creeping protectionism and a place that is coping with globalisation. Above all, it is a region of rising expectations, with young populations and a growing middle class.

How do we collaborate and how do we cooperate in such a region? And how do we deal with the rise of China, and the disputes and tensions between the United States and China? I hope the two speakers will address these topics head-on.

Speech by
Marty Natalegawa[1]

I would like to begin by sharing with you some of my general impressions about the situation that confronts us today. I must emphasise that it might come across as almost a caricature and stands the risk of oversimplification.

First, there is a convergence of the local, national, regional and global. In a way, we are all used to thinking in terms of these different levels, especially those of us who are involved in foreign policy. But convergence between these levels is becoming an increasingly dominant feature. For instance, one may have a phenomenon that begins initially at the local level that quickly spirals out of control to become nationwide, region-wide and global. The most dramatic example of this would be developments in the Middle East. The initial optimism associated with the so-called Arab Spring, taking place at the local level in countries such as Tunisia, quickly enveloped entire countries and then the whole region and beyond, becoming a "perfect storm" of geopolitical tensions.

The second convergence — again, at the risk of oversimplification — is that between the political, economic, security and social domains. While all of us are trained and encouraged to think as if these are clearly identifiable pursuits, as a matter of fact, they affect one another and the resolution of one issue tends to require a holistic and comprehensive perspective of all related issues.

Finally, and not least, is the quality of change. If there is one feature of our world today, it is how change is essentially a permanent condition.

---

[1] The speech was made off-the-cuff. This edited transcript was prepared by the Institute of Policy Studies (IPS). Dr Natalegawa's full remarks are available in video format on the IPS website.

Uncertainty is a given. However, there is an important qualitative difference between recognising uncertainty and being in a state of drift. A state of drift results from the lack of policy coordination. It is a consequence of policy incoherence and policy inconsistencies.

Crucially, the three features that I mentioned — convergence of the local, national, regional and global; convergence of economic, political and social domains; and the element of constant change — have not led to a world that is increasingly more connected. Logic suggests that we should be promoting a greater sense of cooperative partnership, but actually, somewhat worryingly, what we are seeing at the moment is greater divergence. Connectivity of the type I mentioned earlier is not leading to multilateralism and cooperative partnership, but more unilateral tendencies — a "me first" orientation — on the part of countries.

Earlier this morning, Pak George Yeo spoke eloquently of the decline of multilateralism. I would wholeheartedly agree with that, except to add that, in my view, it is not only multilateralism versus unilateralism; it is the entire pursuit of managing issues through diplomacy that appears to be in decline. The art of managing disputes through diplomacy, through communications, is increasingly being lost. We had a time when differences were accepted as a fact of life, but we managed those differences. But now, we have situations where countries differ, but they communicate by means other than diplomacy. Words matter and yet, somehow, words have become increasingly sidelined in the management of relations among nations. This is particularly so in the context of rising geopolitical tensions, especially in our part of the world.

In my view, whether it be countries like Singapore or Indonesia, or regional groupings like ASEAN, we must find a way of managing the nexus, the inter-linkages, between the different layers and the different themes. Unless we have a way of managing them, synergising them in a coherent manner, we will be further challenged as a result.

On geopolitical dynamics, I will not spend much time on the United States (US)-China dimension, because it was extensively discussed this morning. It is a reality that is much recognised. The manifestation is obvious to all of us, whether it be in trade, currency, technology or geopolitics — the South China Sea, the East China Sea, cross-Straits developments, the Korean Peninsula, and so on. The manifestation is crystal clear.

As for the implications for ASEAN, all of us are well aware of how such a push and pull, without an alternative vision from ASEAN, can pull ASEAN apart. But, in my view, the future is not one where one of these sides, either the US or China, will obtain permanent or definitive ascendancy over the other. I think it is a false choice, for us to predict, as if one will be pre-eminent and therefore we must be on the right side of this competition. I believe that the region — as it has been in the past — has defied dominance by any one particular power, and there is no reason to believe that the future will be otherwise.

More importantly, in the 21st century, the nature of power itself has changed. The currency of power is no longer solely military or economic in the traditional sense. Power is more diffused and is more situation-specific. Therefore, when we speak of, say, the US or China, it is not about anticipating which of them will prevail but about readying ourselves for a period of sustained turbulence. One will sometimes obtain an ascendancy over the other in some areas and then, in different situations, vice versa. In other words, for us in the region, we have to be smart in identifying intent, and not to speak of "balance of power" but to speak of "dynamics of power". We should not be too preoccupied with looking at quantitative, measurable capacities, but instead apply ourselves to deciphering intent. This is where diplomacy becomes extremely important, to enable us to truly understand what makes the US and China tick.

My second point on geopolitics is that there are other "bilaterals" out there. Yes, of course, US-China dynamics are extremely important, extremely defining, and of almost existential importance to many countries. But what of US-Russia relations? We are seeing evidence of the return to Cold War dynamics in other parts of the world, but thankfully not quite in this part of the world yet. What of China and Japan? Over the past few weeks, we have begun to see fragile evidence of a potential rapprochement between the two countries. Surely, this is a window of opportunity that ASEAN countries must quickly lock in, or help to lock in. China-Japan relations, be it positive or negative, will have an equally important impact on us, compared to the often discussed US-China relations. What about India-China relations and Japan-Republic of Korea relations? In the past couple of days, we have witnessed some episodes between the two countries. These developments matter to us. In other words, without going through the list, we should broaden our horizon. Let us have instruments to deal not only with US-China relations. We should invest in mechanisms and modalities to deal with all these other "bilaterals" that will be confronting us in the future.

This leads me to the last segment of my remarks, which has to do with the policy response by ASEAN. In my view, passivism is not a smart option for ASEAN. ASEAN, in the past, had demonstrated its capacity to be transformative. The formation of ASEAN itself in 1967, for instance, the Treaty of Amity and Cooperation (TAC) in 1976, the expansion of ASEAN, and the ASEAN Community project all have one overriding quality — the quality of a can-do spirit. ASEAN leaders did not simply take the situation as it was but had a bit more of an aspirational and transformative outlook and were often ahead of their time. Sometimes, the moves proved to be redundant, to be not quite what was needed, but we could not be accused of being passive.

Even in our so-called external affairs, ASEAN was growing in confidence, initially in promoting the idea of neutrality for Southeast Asia. The original Zone of Peace, Freedom and Neutrality (ZOPFAN) idea spoke of Southeast Asia as being neutralised. Imagine that, it is an active term. We were seeking to have countries neutralise us because the world was too complicated, and we did not want to be torn apart. But then, we went on to develop the idea of resilience for the region. We developed the more ambitious idea of centrality. The vehicles are well known, for instance, the ASEAN Plus Three, the ASEAN Plus Group, the ASEAN Regional Forum, and the East Asian Summit process.

My point is that ASEAN has demonstrated that it has more to offer than just its convening power. We created a home for countries to meet and to deliberate, but more than simply being an efficient event organiser, we also provided intellectual and geopolitical leadership. We shaped and moulded the TAC, and that was externalised. We pushed the non-ASEAN countries into a competitive benign dynamic to compete with one another — to outdo one another — to accede to the TAC.

I believe we can do more of this. The Indo-Pacific notion, for instance, that is now much talked about, is actually provided for within the East Asia Summit. I recall that when we first discussed the various permutations of the East Asia Summit back in the early 2000s, it was a lengthy debate, but we eventually formed the East Asia Summit, which included countries like India,

Australia and New Zealand. We were clearly, inherently and purposefully Indo-Pacific in our outlook.

Now, I return to my point on ASEAN's policy response at this critical and very extremely uncertain juncture. Asking very general "meaning-of-life" questions about what is the Indo-Pacific and what is not the Indo-Pacific is not useful. Instead, we should empower the East Asian Summit, and then we can really deliver on ASEAN centrality. Because we already have it. All the countries, and the principles of the Indo-Pacific, are in the East Asia Summit. The ASEAN Regional Forum, which we already have, also contains many countries of both the Pacific and the Indian Ocean. But we need to deliver on substance.

We need to make it worthwhile for leaders to come to our capitals every year, beyond discussing procedural issues. On empowering forums such as the East Asia Summit, I believe ASEAN must be crystal clear in identifying what the nature of the problems are, otherwise we will have wonderful proposals and suggestions looking for problems. The problems must be identified before we come to the instruments. In my view, the key problems include the trust deficit amongst nations and the lack of crisis management capacity in this part of the world. I mentioned earlier that there was an episode between Japan and the Republic of Korea, and an episode elsewhere involving countries of Northeast Asia, and yet, there is a lacuna of action and a time-sensitive forum that can discuss these developments. We have to wait for the next scheduled meeting towards the end of the year in the case of the East Asia Summit. Things happen during the year. We cannot wait for the summit at the end of the year before we can begin to discuss these matters.

All in all, it is a challenging environment. But ASEAN had, in the past, whenever doubts were raised about its continued relevance, managed to reinvent itself and prove its relevance. Over the past year, Singapore has not only chaired ASEAN, it has also shown tremendous leadership of ASEAN, introducing new areas of cooperation hitherto absent, which is a mark of leadership for member states of ASEAN.

SESSION

Speech by
Bilahari Kausikan[1]

Singapore is in Southeast Asia. This is a geographical fact. But although we are *in* Southeast Asia, we are not always *of* Southeast Asia — and we cannot be. There are three key factors that make Singapore something of an anomaly in Southeast Asia and prescribe why we must always be something of an outlier in Southeast Asia, even though we are part of the region.

The first factor is an ethnic one. Singapore is an ethnic Chinese majority sovereign state, in fact, the only one in the world outside Greater China. But Southeast Asia is a region where the Chinese are not always a welcomed minority. Secondly, although we are an ethnic Chinese majority state, Singapore is organised horizontally on the basis of multiracial meritocracy. Now, multiracial meritocracy in Singapore is not perfect, but there is no perfection to be found on earth. It is nevertheless a principle that we take seriously. And we live in a region where every other state is either formally or informally organised on a very different principle, and that principle is an ethnic or religious hierarchy — or both. You know all the examples.

In Malaysia, ethnic hierarchy is enshrined as a formal part of the constitution — Article 153. Indonesia's formal organising ideology is Pancasila, which is, in theory, horizontal, but the informal hierarchy of *pribumi* over *non-pribumi* is the political reality. You can say the same of almost any other country. In Thailand, it is the ethnic Thai Buddhist over the Malay Muslim in the south. In Myanmar, it is the ethnic Burman Buddhist over the Rohingya and other minorities. And this is true of the broader region in

---

[1] The speech was made off-the-cuff. This edited transcript was prepared by the Institute of Policy Studies (IPS). Mr Kausikan's full remarks are available in video format on the IPS website.

Southeast Asia. In China, it is clearly a hierarchy of the Han over the non-Han. Even in Japan, which is a liberal democracy, it is clearly a hierarchy of the ethnic Japanese over, say, the Japanese citizens of Korean or Chinese descent.

Together, these two factors have historically led to Singapore being regarded with a certain degree of suspicion by other countries in the region. The suspicion at one time was that we were a "Third China", and other countries projected a great deal of their suspicions of China and their attitudes towards their own ethnic Chinese minorities onto Singapore. So, after independence, the Singapore government devoted a great deal of energy and effort trying to dispel this perception of Singapore. I think, as far as the governments of Southeast Asia are concerned, we have been largely successful. I do not think any *government* in Southeast Asia thinks of us as a Third China, and they understand that there is now a distinct Singapore identity, separate from the various ethnic identities. But those are the attitudes of the governments. I am less confident that the attitudes of the *populations* of other Southeast Asian countries have changed. Perhaps they will in time, but I do not think we are there yet.

At the same time, there is a complication here. The attitudes of Southeast Asia towards China have changed. It is no longer one of unmitigated suspicion. But the change has not been complete or entire. Some of you may know of a recent ISEAS-Yusof Ishak Institute survey that revealed that, while it is broadly acknowledged that China is an important and influential actor in Southeast Asia, this perception coexists with significant scepticism about China. What this means is that the emergence and the acceptance of a distinct Singapore identity separate from the ethnic composition of Singapore is not to be taken for granted and has to be maintained by the conscious efforts of policy. In fact, I think this is so even internally within Singapore because — do not forget — we are only 54 years old, and that is not a very long time in the history of a country. Singapore is a young nation, and while acceptance of a distinct Singapore identity is real and an important development, I suspect this identity is still relatively shallow and therefore malleable.

A further complication is the fact that US-China relations have clearly entered into a new long-term phase of heightened strategic competition. This adds significantly to the complexity of the region and the complexity of countries' decisions on how to position themselves in the midst of this great power competition — the obvious manifestation of which is the trade war. But the term "trade war" is something of a misnomer because trade is an instrument; the objective is strategic competition. Another factor that cautions against taking a distinct Singapore identity for granted is the resurgence of what is generally known as populism, but I think it is more accurately described as the politics of nativism or indigeneity in key countries in Southeast Asia, and this is part of a global trend that shows no sign of abating. By the way, Singapore, too, is not unaffected by this trend, although what we have seen here is, as yet, a fairly mild form of it.

Now, the third factor that makes Singapore unique in Southeast Asia is the fact that we are a city-state with no natural hinterland within our sovereign territory. Now, a small city-state cannot take its international relevance or even its regional relevance for granted. Relevance is an artefact that has to be created by human endeavour and, having been created, has to be maintained by human endeavour. What does this mean? What is the implication of having to create and sustain relevance for yourself? What is the implication of being something of an anomaly in Southeast Asia?

It means that, while Singapore is in Southeast Asia as a geographical fact, we must always look beyond Southeast Asia to make a living and to ensure our security. This is a strategic imperative. Another way of stating the same point is that we have to be different. We have to be extraordinary. We have to leverage our difference, in order to be extraordinary. We cannot be just like any other country in Southeast Asia for the simple reason that, if we were just like any other country in Southeast Asia, why would anybody want to deal with us, rather than our larger neighbours who are endowed with natural resources?

We have to acknowledge that there is a certain tension between these imperatives — between the imperative to be extraordinary and the fact that we are in Southeast Asia. If we were just like anybody else, we would soon find ourselves at risk of irrelevance. Being extraordinary does not necessarily make us universally loved, but it cannot be helped. That is the existential condition of being Singaporean.

Now, what are we to do about this? First, the management of these complexities depends first of all on ourselves, to maintain what makes us unique and, in particular, how we organise ourselves as a society on the basis of multiracial meritocracy. If we can do that, I think we can manage the other complexities. If we cannot do that, we are done for. Do not forget: We live in an era where identities of various kinds — "nativisms" of different kinds and "indigeneities" of different kinds — are being asserted globally, and I do not see why we should be exempted from these global trends.

The second point is that ASEAN is a vital and irreplaceable means of managing the tensions that I mentioned. There is no substitute. Pak Marty Natalegawa here has written a very good book on ASEAN — *Does ASEAN Matter? A View from Within* — which I commend to all of you. All of you should read it. Pak will no doubt speak in greater detail on ASEAN, as he is, in many ways, Mr ASEAN. I leave that to him.

I will just end by saying that, while ASEAN is, and must remain, central to Singapore's foreign policy, it is a tool, one of many. There are things that ASEAN can do and does very well, but there are some things that ASEAN cannot do or will have limitations in what it is able to do. We should never lose sight of this fact. It is a vital tool, an irreplaceable tool, but it is still one tool. It is not a panacea for all the ills in the world, all the ills of Singapore, and all the ills of the region. It would be dangerous for Singapore and Singaporeans to confuse a very useful and vital tool for some kind of magic nostrum that cures everything.

IV

Speech by
Vivian Balakrishnan, Minister
for Foreign Affairs, Singapore

Speech by
Vivian Balakrishnan[1]

Let me first say that, if you ignore the rest of my speech, I only ask you to remember three phrases: first, Fractured World Order; second, Fractious Domestic Politics; and third, Digital Disruption. What I am going to attempt to show today is a chain of causality between these three elements.

Let me start by stating the obvious. We live in a very uncertain, volatile and difficult world. You have heard discussions on the strategic tensions between China and the United States (US) — I would include Russia here. You have also heard, or you would be aware, that politics as we know it is over. In fact, mainstream politicians all over the world are in trouble, and we are witnessing the simultaneous rise of both right-wing and left-wing populism — all over the world, not just in the West.

You are aware that there is deep anxiety the world over, especially among the middle class, over wage stagnation and the future of jobs. We are also painfully aware that there is anger over increasing inequality. If that were not enough, I would hasten to add that the level of carbon dioxide in the air is more than 400 parts per million. The last time the world had carbon dioxide at these levels was at least 400,000 years ago. And since I am a doctor, I can tell you that we are overdue for the next pandemic.

---

[1] The official transcript of this speech is on the website of the Ministry of Foreign Affairs (www.mfa.gov.sg). This version has been edited by IPS for the purposes of inclusion in this publication. The full speech is available in video format on the IPS website.

PROPOSITION

So, having put you all in a good mood — my thesis today is that we are witnessing a Fractured World Order, due to Fractious Domestic Politics, that is caused by a Digital Disruption. This is a chain of causality. Let me restate this chain. I believe that technology is a key driving force of human progress. And the early masters of technology accumulate and wield outsize power — financial, political and, ultimately, military. Hence, every time the world experiences a major technological breakthrough, there will be, by definition, revolutionary shifts in the economic means of production. And when you get changes in means of economic production, that in turn will disrupt society and change politics. This, in turn, will alter the global balance of power. We have seen all this before, it is just that this is about to be replayed, but at a faster pace, by different actors.

INDUSTRIAL REVOLUTION

Let me start with the Industrial Revolution, to give you some empirical evidence. We are speaking English today because the Industrial Revolution started in England. Thomas Savery and Thomas Newcomen invented the steam engine. This was later improved upon by James Watt. The steam engine replaced animal and human labour with energy from fossil fuels.

What this meant was the beginning of mechanisation. It uprooted the economy. Previously handcrafted products were now mass produced. And, importantly, owning capital became far more lucrative than just owning land. It transformed agrarian societies. Bear in mind that human beings have had agricultural societies for 8,000 years. In turn, now that you have machines and factories, you need labour. Labour migrated to urban centres, and you get urbanisation and cities. Increasingly, in the political field, power structures shifted from the land owners in feudal societies to owners of capital in industrial capitalist societies.

The way labour was exploited in the early phase of the Industrial Revolution, the vicissitudes of work, and the impact of losing a job in those days, in turn generated a social and political backlash. And that is why we have today's trade unions and the welfare state in Europe. These were, in a sense, the political response to the last Industrial Revolution, and this was how the modern political order (with right and left wings) emerged — from massive socio-economic disruption driven by the advent of mechanised production.

What did this mean for us in the Industrial age? Industrial Britain needed raw materials, a lot of which were from Southeast Asia, and new markets. Trade expeditions were sent out, the navy was strengthened, and outposts established — including, exactly 200 years ago to this day, Singapore, where Raffles landed to establish an outpost. The outcome of this trade and foreign policy was an empire on which the sun never set, and pre-eminence for Great Britain for more than a century.

FORDISM

What happened after that? The next breakthrough was the concept of a moving assembly line. The archetypical example of that happened in the US, with Henry Ford's Model T car. Mass production was made possible through task specialisation. What used to take 12 hours to produce — a car, now took 2 hours and 30 minutes. Prices fell, and a virtuous cycle between mass production and mass consumption was created. Those workers that Henry Ford employed, who earned high wages, could now become consumers in their own right. So we now witnessed capital and wealth accumulating, even more than before. Those who are interested in history will know there was a period called the "Gilded Age", and that there were "robber barons" who found ways to enrich themselves. It was a period of increasing inequality.

Across the globe, reactionary responses to this type of asymmetric capital accumulation led to growing extremism — fascists on the right and communists on the left. Economic rivalry and political miscalculations sowed the seeds for the two world wars of the last century.

FOREIGN POLICY

The corollary, of course, was that the US, having outdone all other countries in technological superiority, was actually the undisputed main winner of World War II and emerged as a global superpower. Yes, I know there was a distraction of more than 50 years of the Cold War. But, in a sense, there was no question that the US had technological supremacy. We should not have been surprised by the fall of the Berlin Wall.

The US' share of global Gross Domestic Product (GDP) in 1960 was around 40 per cent. Today, although the US GDP has continued to grow, on a relative scale, it is now about 24 per cent. And, you realise, when a single superpower has 40 per cent of global GDP, for every dollar created in the world, 40 cents accumulates to it. In that scenario, it was worthwhile for the US to set the rules of global engagement, and to be the primary architect and underwriter of the world order that has existed since the end of World War II. This was the system defined by free markets, free trade, and global economic integration.

Along the way, the United Nations (UN) was formed, along with the Bretton Woods Institutions (International Monetary Fund and World Bank), World Trade Organization (WTO), the Marshall Plan for Europe, and the reconstruction of Japan. The GI Bill provided mass education for veterans, which gave them the skills to harvest the fruits of the Industrial Revolution. There was, therefore, a Golden Age for capitalism for about 30 or 35 years after the end of World War II — an age of a rising middle class, which could afford a house and home, and the security to provide for their families. The foundations of the rules-based multilateral system, in fact, gave newly independent countries like Singapore a small seat at the table and significant opportunities.

POST-WAR GLOBALISATION

Think about the process of globalisation that occurred after the war. In fact, it was again driven by the technological revolution. Think of names like William Shockley, John Bardeen and Walter Brattain, who invented the transistor in 1947. But it was Dick Morley's Programmable Logic Controller that revolutionised industrial control, because it made it easier to reprogramme machinery in factories and change products in accordance with consumer needs. Now that production was easily adjusted, improvements in shipping logistics and, at the same time, the explosion in Information and Communications Technology (ICT), transformed the world once again. At its zenith was just-in-time production, which allowed global supply chains to be constructed. Multinational companies, or MNCs, became a formidable force, very often having revenues exceeding that of small countries.

Now, think about Singapore's position in the mid-1960s when we were unexpectedly thrust into independence. Fortunately, our early leaders chose to do what was unfashionable in the early post-colonial era — they invited these same MNCs that were building global supply chains to bring their technology and access to markets to us. This was unconventional back in the 1960s. Other countries, newly independent, were focused on import substitution. So, paradoxically, because Singapore lost its hinterland and because we had to invite the MNCs, we became a global city way before the word "globalisation" became fashionable. We moved up the value chain, into advanced manufacturing and, ultimately, global services. Our GDP grew from US$500 per capita in 1965 to more than US$50,000 per capita 53 years later.

As Dr Goh Keng Swee said, we needed the humility to learn, the courage to be unconventional, and the ability to unify and carry our people as we embarked on this journey. Today, the success of Singapore is a living testament to the fruits of an export-oriented, free-market capitalist system. We have fully exploited our improved air, sea and digital links in an increasingly connected world.

But the point is this: We were in the right time, right place, with the right technology and right strategy. It is important, therefore, to understand that we cannot engage in navel-gazing, but that we need to understand what is happening around us, and then adjust our posture. Now, whilst the net impact of globalisation has clearly been positive for Singapore, in a sense, actually, we had no choice.

Nevertheless, we must be careful not to overstate the benefits of globalisation. The political reality is that, with globalisation and automation, there will always be winners and losers. For Singapore, as a relatively young country, we started from a low base and made a quantum leap up, due to the visionary political leadership that we had. So we are clear winners in this age of globalisation. But in the western world, especially in the last 30 years, it is clear that a significant number of people, especially blue-collar workers, have been left behind. Blue-collar workers in Europe and in the West more generally, have seen their wages stagnate, jobs move overseas, and their income gap with the elite widen, and they are increasingly aggrieved. In a sense, this is another upheaval, another backlash, and we should not have been surprised by it.

RISE OF SMART TECHNOLOGY

Now, to make things more complicated — and we have not even digested the full consequences of the last Industrial Revolution — well, to compound matters, a new digital revolution is upon us. This time, it is the rise of smart technology, and in particular, smart technology due to machine learning, a phenomenon which has only really taken off in the last two or three years. If you were a biologist, you would say, well, you tried to copy the brain, where you have multiple layers of synapses, simple on their own, but by making connections, you create systems that are able to recognise patterns. But this would not have been possible without the exponential rise in computing power, networks, big data and new algorithms. I want to say, as a biologist, as a doctor, that pattern recognition is the difference between artificial intelligence (AI), smart AI, and standard automation. The ability to recognise patterns is the basis for vision, for listening, for speaking, for translation, and for cognition.

For example, Google developed the Alpha Go programme, which beat human professional Go player, Lee Sedol, without handicaps in 2016 for the first time. I often find that Western audiences who have not played the game of Go may not realise how complex the game is. There are more combinations of moves in Go than there are atoms in the universe. What this means is that, unlike chess or Sudoku, it cannot be solved via standard rules-based programming. Let me tell you, since Prime Minister Lee Hsien Loong has programmed a Sudoku solver in "C", which I translated into Javascript, I can attest that Go has a completely different level of complexity.

So, for the first time in human history, not only has human and animal energy been replaced by fossil fuels, not only have automation and globalisation taken over, but now, robotics, machine learning and AI are already revolutionising the finance, commerce, defence, logistics, health and transport sectors.

Now, just to give you an idea of how much progress has occurred in the last two years. In 2016, the UN uploaded about 800,000 documents to the internet. The critical feature of that upload was that the UN has six official languages and so it uploaded documents which were translated word for word by humans in six different languages. In 2016, at the same time that

Google was playing Go, it decided to use the same techniques of machine learning to do translation. Any one of you who has used Google Translate before 2016 and today would know that there is a big difference. The big difference was that they shifted over to machine learning, neural nets, and pattern recognition. When Google did it, they did not tell anybody. They kept it a secret, until a Japanese researcher in November of that year started to notice that Google Translate had improved, and then they revealed their "secret sauce". In fact, they had stopped all development using old techniques and switched over to machine learning.

Now, there is another explosion occurring, and that is in 5G technology, and I do not just mean the contest between the US and China. 5G will create unprecedented levels of connectivity. It will increase bandwidth, it will explode the Internet of Things, and there will be a tsunami of data. Pattern recognition and machine learning depend on data, and you now have a tsunami of data, and the algorithms, computing power, and networks to deal with it. You are sitting on a real revolutionary technology.

Language barriers will erode. But herein lies another problem. It means that you are now competing not only with workers overseas, not only with machines locally, but that telepresence is now multilingual. There are only about a billion people who speak English to a sufficient level to perform useful technical work today. But once you break these barriers of language, you can easily double or triple that number.

The point is that we are going to see disrupted societies and fractious politics, and the global order as we know it is going to change. In fact, there will be considerable dislocation because the pace of change is accelerating. And in the example I gave you, I bet most people in this room were not aware of how much has changed in just the last two years. If history is a guide, every time you get a change like this, you get an initial "Gilded Age", greater inequality, and "robber barons" — the early masters and adopters of technology. And it takes time before the new means of production are democratised and a new middle class can arise.

I believe we are now in a new digital "Gilded Age". There are winners, and there are losers. The winners are the supranational technology companies — you know the names — Google, Amazon, Apple and Facebook, which are growing in economic and political clout. Why? Because they sit on mountains of specific and very often personal data. And there are losers — those who have not been able to skill up and have lost their jobs due to disruptive changes. Automation in the past took away many blue-collar jobs. But pattern recognition of today and tomorrow could also make many white-collar jobs redundant. It is true that new jobs will be created — my worry is that this will not be fast enough to replace the old jobs, and this will cause further dislocation and fractious domestic politics.

We are already seeing the political effects — increasing polarisation and a hollowing out of the centre of the middle class and of mainstream politics. We see that in virtually all societies, one group is moving further Right — channelling frustration towards immigrants and free trade. They want to build walls. Another group is moving further to the Left — demanding increased subsidies, one example of which is Universal Basic Income, and they want radical redistribution. Can you see it? The collapse of the centre, and the rise of the right wing and the left wing. This breakdown of domestic consensus will inevitably disrupt the international system.

There will be countries that are afraid of change and fear competition, that will question the value of the current liberal world order. On the other hand, nations like Singapore believe we need to master the new technologies, face competition head on, double down on interdependence, integration and openness, and seek win-win collaboration. The division and divergence will grow more acute as technological adoption accelerates. This is our current predicament.

US-CHINA TECHNOLOGICAL CONTEST

The US-China technological contest is a case in point. China's achievements in the last 40 years since its reform and opening up (改革开放, *gaige kaifang*) have been astounding. It has lifted 800 million out of poverty since 1990. Its GDP per capita has risen from US$90 in 1960 to over US$8,000 in 2016. China has climbed up the technological value chain. Today, we have all heard about companies like Tencent, Alibaba and Huawei. This is not just catch-up industrialisation, this is leading-edge, cutting-edge technology.

In the earlier period, the US and China had a mutually beneficial and interdependent relationship, very different from the relationship between the US and Russia during the Cold War. You had US companies flocking to China, and China became part of their global supply chains. The US welcomed Chinese investments and talent. Trade in goods and services reached over US$700 billion per annum. But today, the nature of relations is shifting from engagement to strategic competition. The question is, why?

China has used the last four decades of reform and opening up to catch up on the last Industrial Revolution. The question now is who will master smart technology, AI, robotics and big data first — who will be better able to acquire and apply the data, techniques and tools better, faster, and more effectively. Countries used to compete over land and capital, but today, the fight is going to be over data. Data will be the crucial factor of production in this brave new world. And the one who acquires and applies the most data will have an enormous advantage, an enormous head start. In this technological contest, the stakes are actually even higher than they were in the past. Why? Precisely because in the digital arena, global markets — geography itself — have contracted.

Let me just give you an example. When the Silk Road first started, the price of silk in Europe was 10,000 times the price of silk in Beijing. Why? Because transportation, logistics, were so difficult. Today, in a world with fibre, Amazon, e-commerce, and the rest of it, those kinds of differentials have collapsed. What this means is that if you have the best silk, the best product, you have access to a global market. The consequences of winning, especially as we move towards a winner-takes-all world, are profound. There is an enormous difference between being "Number One" and "Number Two".

We see this contest in the race among the major powers to become the world leader in 5G networks. I am not downplaying the other areas of strategic contest, such as in trade. But we need to recognise that something more fundamental is at work here. Even if the US and China manage to settle their current trade disputes — which Singapore obviously earnestly hopes that they will — things will not be hunky-dory.

Because of the pervasiveness of technology, we expect this strategic contest to be waged in other arenas — in defence, energy, cybersecurity and outer space. Alongside the contest for technological mastery runs a parallel contest for governance. The question is: Whose preferred paradigm will regulate the emerging global commons such as cyberspace and outer space? Should these be democratised, or subject to the free market, or state-controlled? These are not easy questions to answer. We took many years to reach a global consensus on regulating the high seas and international trade. That is why we have the UN Convention on the Law of the Sea (UNCLOS) and the WTO. Discussions on cyberspace and outer space regulations are still in the very nascent stages.

How should we in Singapore respond to such a world? In this age, smart technologies and big data hold the keys to the future. The ones with the keys will retain economic and geopolitical relevance, and shape global rules. But the runners-up will not just be incrementally disadvantaged. They will be left exponentially further behind. It is this technological contest and its impact on the economy that underpins the conduct of foreign policy. The cut and thrust of politics may dominate our attention from day to day but, in reality, they are mere froth atop tectonic shifts in the geostrategic balance of power.

HOW SHOULD SINGAPORE RESPOND?

What is a small country like Singapore to do in this brave new world we find ourselves in? Singapore's foreign policy principles remain as salient today as they were in 1965. In a word, it has always boiled down to relevance. In 2009, Mr Lee Kuan Yew delivered the S Rajaratnam Lecture. He said, "We must make ourselves relevant so that other countries have an interest in our continued survival and prosperity as a sovereign and independent nation. Singapore cannot take its relevance for granted. Small countries perform no vital or irreplaceable functions in the international system. Singapore has to continually reconstruct itself and keep its relevance to the world and to create political and economic space." These words are still absolutely relevant today.

So, what should we do? First, Singapore must always remain open; open for business and open especially to talent. We must maintain a society that is fair, maintain our reputation for integrity, and remain trusted by all. We are a small country with no natural resources. We cannot try to build walls to shelter our population, because hiding from inevitable change is not a survival strategy. So our doors, by definition, must remain open to all who wish to engage us and, in fact, we must actively create the conditions that will attract others to keep coming. We will continue to strengthen our air, sea and digital connectivity, deepening our economic and investment links with partners across the globe. One of my favourite pictures is the map of submarine cables, which carry data, the currency of the future, and are the "new Maritime Silk Road".[2] We must entrench Singapore's hub status in these new communications routes.

Just as we protected and treated the investments of MNCs and even the oil that was stored in tanks in Singapore carefully, for data, we must remain helpful, neutral and reliable. Our legal framework will continue to respond to these emerging technologies. We will have to have safeguards in place to protect intellectual property, data and privacy. As I said before, our reputation for integrity, reliability and straight talking is critical. We do not wish to be compelled to choose sides — I know this is a standard question and I will always be asked about this. We do not wish to be asked to choose sides in this strategic and technological contest, because we believe that synergies will be more powerful when we cooperate to create common rather than competing growth platforms. This core belief informs our approach to global governance.

This brings me to my second point, that Singapore will always work to fortify the multilateral system and contribute actively to the shaping of new norms to govern the global commons. Our role in this has been established, with Ambassador Tommy Koh playing a leading role in finalising UNCLOS, the "constitution for the seas", and with our Climate Change negotiators — I had personally spent four and a half years trying, in our own way, to play an outsized role to seal the Paris Agreement for climate change.

I have spoken about the current debate over cyberspace and outer space regulation. Singapore's position on this is unequivocal — all must be involved in shaping the new rules and the concerns of small states must be taken on board. Arriving at a consensus will not be easy, given that the stakes are high, but it is precisely because of this that new norms are necessary. And Singapore can always be counted on to send our best people to these international expert groups and negotiations so that we can make a positive, constructive contribution.

Third, we need to continue to diversify our partnerships. Technological disruption will erode borders, revolutionise business models, and shift production bases. New technology hubs will emerge. No advantage is

---

[2] A map of submarine cables connecting Singapore to the rest of the world is available here: www.submarinecablemap.com/#/country/singapore (as of 15 March 2019)

engraved in stone. We should move away from conventional markets and "safe models" to capitalise on new opportunities — some of which are right at our doorstep.

ASEAN is a dynamic region, with a rising middle class, and boundless potential for the next few decades at least. More than half of ASEAN's population is under the age of 30, and many are digital natives. The 2018 e-Conomy Southeast Asia report by Google and Temasek described the growth of our region's internet economy as record-breaking. Our region's internet economy reached US$72 billion in 2018, more than doubling from 2015. Therefore, we believe it is essential to build thicker and deeper linkages across ASEAN cities, and to create new partnerships as we get onto these new technology ladders. Other countries and corporations are hungry to engage us, and we should reciprocate enthusiastically.

This is why we established the ASEAN Smart Cities Network under Singapore's ASEAN Chairmanship last year, as a first step in this direction. I am pleased that it was extremely well-received by our neighbours. Twenty-six pilot cities developed action plans from 2018 till 2025, and several of these projects have attracted partnerships between the private sector and the state sector. In future, the development of technology will not be driven top-down by state institutions, but by a trilateral collaboration between the state, the private sector and consumers. I am very proud that ASEAN has taken a step towards harnessing this productive dynamic.

CONCLUSION

Let me conclude by saying that we live in extraordinary times. Not every generation gets to live through a revolution, but we are living through one now. Entire multi-billion dollar industries exist because technologies are changing in front of our eyes. If you think about the explosion in apps and services that are being generated, the pace is only going to accelerate.

Disruption brings challenges, but also opportunities. We recognise that Singapore, by dint of our size, will never be a global superpower. But we can and we must master technology if we are to remain successful, and preserve our independence to make decisions based on our own sovereign interests in this coming age. By playing our cards right, we can remain in a sweet spot, just as we have for the last five decades. We have done it before, by catching the offshoring wave when we industrialised in the 1960s. In the 1970s, we bet on the right horse by doubling down on logistics management with our container port and airports. We then moved on to electronics in the 1980s. We can do it again with big data and smart technology.

To do so, Singapore must continue to remain open, engaging all who wish to be friends and partners with us. We must strengthen our "convening power" not only for meetings like last year's US-DPRK Summit, but we must be the best place for any MNC to assemble a multinational team in the world. Regardless of where people come from, this is a convenient, safe, beautiful and conducive place for them and their families to live and work in multinational teams.

We must continue to engage all major powers, but do so in a disciplined and principled way, and preserve our neutrality. I sometimes remind everyone that this is why, from time to time, Singapore must have the ability to say "no" to our neighbours, to say "no" even to the superpowers — not as a capricious exercise, but in a principled and disciplined way, to prove our neutrality and that we are worthy of people's trust. Our history has shown that we can work with all parties and partners, to create common space and pursue mutually beneficial outcomes. We will concurrently work to uphold international law and the rules-based international order, even in the new global commons of cyberspace and outer space. We are committed to ensuring that the multilateral framework, which has underpinned our peace and prosperity, continues to be preserved and remains relevant.

To bring this all home, we need Singaporeans to be fully prepared to collectively face this new age of disruption. Since independence, Singapore has relied on our people's ingenuity and tenacity, and willingness to sacrifice and do whatever it takes to survive and thrive. The times we live in require us to double down on these attributes of Singaporeans. If we do not ride this next wave of technology, we will sink under it. This is why economic restructuring is a key priority for the Singapore government. This is why we will continue to improve our education system, and our retraining and upskilling schemes, such as SkillsFuture. This has to be not just a word, but a critical and inherent part of our strategy for survival, to enable Singaporeans to master technology.

We will adjust our social security system in a fiscally sustainable way to give Singaporeans confidence to navigate these disruptive times. The government will do our part to equip and prepare Singaporeans, even as we explore new markets, build new partnerships, facilitate new business models, and harness new technologies. Companies and individuals now need to be entrepreneurial and adventurous.

We must be able to seize new opportunities and remain resilient in the time to come. If we succeed, we will navigate safely through this current Gilded Age, and a new Golden Age awaits us.

About the Speakers

BALAKRISHNAN, Vivian is the Minister for Foreign Affairs and the Minister-in-charge of the Smart Nation initiative. He has previously held appointments as the Minister for the Environment and Water Resources, Minister for Community Development, Youth and Sports, Second Minister for Trade and Industry, Minister responsible for Entrepreneurship, Second Minister for Information, Communications and the Arts and Minister of State for National Development. Before becoming a Member of Parliament in 2001, he was Chief Executive Officer of the Singapore General Hospital. He became Medical Director of the Singapore National Eye Centre in 1999, having studied Medicine at the National University of Singapore after being awarded the President's Scholarship in 1980, and specialised in ophthalmology after graduation.

CHAN Heng Chee is Ambassador-at-Large at the Ministry of Foreign Affairs of Singapore and Chairman of the Lee Kuan Yew Centre for Innovative Cities at the Singapore University of Technology and Design. She is Chairman of the National Arts Council, member of the Presidential Council for Minority Rights, and Co-Chair of the Asia Society Board of Trustees. She was Singapore's Representative on the ASEAN Inter-governmental Commission on Human Rights (2012–2015). She served as Ambassador to the United States (1996–2012) and Permanent Representative to the United Nations in New York (1989–1991), concurrently High Commissioner to Canada and Ambassador to Mexico. She was previously Head of the Political Science Department at the National University of Singapore, founding Director of the Institute of Policy Studies, and Director of the Institute of Southeast Asian Studies.

CHNG Kai Fong is Managing Director of Singapore's Economic Development Board. He was Principal Private Secretary to Prime Minister Lee Hsien Loong (2014–2017). Previously, he was Director of Communications Group at the Prime Minister's Office, where he oversaw strategic communications and coordinated communications strategy across government agencies, Director of Resource Industry at the Ministry of Trade and Industry, and Director of the Institute of Public Sector Leadership. Mr Chng has also served in the Ministry of Home Affairs and the Ministry of Communications and Information. He was seconded from the Singapore government to Shell to serve as a Senior Management Consultant in its Downstream Strategy Division from 2008 to 2010.

DEVAN, Janadas, Director of the Institute of Policy Studies, was educated at the National University of Singapore and Cornell University in the United States. He was a journalist, writing for *The Straits Times* and broadcasting for Radio Singapore International, before being appointed the Government's Chief of Communications at the Ministry of Communications and Information in 2012. He is concurrently Deputy Secretary at the Prime Minister's Office.

KAUSIKAN, Bilahari is Chairman of the Middle East Institute of the National University of Singapore. He was Ambassador-at-Large at the Ministry of Foreign Affairs of Singapore from 2013 to 2018. Prior to that, from 2001 to 2013, Mr Kausikan was the second Permanent Secretary and then Permanent Secretary at the Ministry of Foreign Affairs. He was Ambassador to the Russian Federation (1994–1995) and Permanent Representative to the United Nations in New York (1995–1998), concurrently High Commissioner to Canada, and Ambassador to Mexico. As the Institute of Policy Studies' 2nd S R Nathan Fellow, he delivered a series of lectures on Singapore's foreign policy, which were collected and published in his book, *Dealing with an Ambiguous World*.

KOH, Tommy is Ambassador-at-Large at the Ministry of Foreign Affairs of Singapore and Special Adviser to the Institute of Policy Studies. He is also the Chairman of the Governing Board at the Centre for International Law and Rector of Tembusu College at the National University of Singapore; and

Co-Chair of the China-Singapore Forum and the Japan-Singapore Symposium. He was Chairman of the National Arts Council and National Heritage Board. He was previously Ambassador to the United States, Permanent Representative to the United Nations in New York, High Commissioner to Canada and Ambassador to Mexico. He was President of the Third UN Conference on the Law of the Sea, Chairman of the 1992 Earth Summit, served as the UN Secretary-General's Special Envoy to Russia, Estonia, Latvia and Lithuania, and was Singapore's Chief Negotiator for the US-Singapore Free Trade Agreement.

LEE Chee Koon is President and Group Chief Executive Officer at CapitaLand Limited. He was previously CapitaLand's Group Chief Investment Officer. He joined CapitaLand in 2007 as Vice President for Office of the President. He held various appointments in The Ascott Limited, CapitaLand's serviced residence business, before serving as Chief Executive Officer (2013–2018). Prior to joining CapitaLand, he had served in the Ministry of Trade and Industry, Ministry of Finance, and Monetary Authority of Singapore. In 2016, Mr Lee was conferred the National Order of Merit (Chevalier de l'Ordre National du Mérite) by the President of the French Republic for Ascott's contributions to France. Mr Lee was presented with the Business China Young Achiever Award in 2017 by Prime Minister Lee Hsien Loong for Ascott's contributions to Singapore-China relations.

LIM, Gabriel is Permanent Secretary at the Ministry of Communications and Information of Singapore. Prior to this, he was Chief Executive Officer of the Info-communications Media Development Authority (IMDA). Before his appointment at IMDA, Mr Lim had been Principal Private Secretary to Prime Minister Lee Hsien Loong (2011–2014) and Director (Policy) at the Defence Policy Office of the Ministry of Defence. His earlier postings in the Singapore government include the Ministry of Health, Public Service Division and Civil Service College. Mr Lim serves on the Board of Directors for the National Healthcare Group, National Research Foundation, SGInnovate, CapitaLand Limited, Civil Service College, St Joseph's Institution International, and St Joseph's Institution International Elementary School.

NATALEGAWA, Marty is a member of the United Nations Secretary-General's High-Level Advisory Board on Mediation, member of the Board of Trustees of the International Crisis Group, and a Distinguished Fellow of the Asia Policy Institute. Dr Natalegawa had a distinguished career in diplomacy. He was Indonesia's Minister of Foreign Affairs from 2009 to 2014. Prior to that, he was Permanent Representative to the UN in New York (2007–2009), during which he was President of the UN Security Council in 2007. He was a member of the UN Secretary-General's High-Level Panel on Global Response to Health Crises (2015). He was Ambassador to the United Kingdom and Ireland (2005–2007). Dr Natalegawa's book, *Does ASEAN Matter? A View from Within*, was published by ISEAS - Yusof Ishak Institute of Singapore in 2018.

WANG Gungwu is University Professor at the National University of Singapore and Emeritus Professor at the Australian National University. He is former President of the Australian Academy of the Humanities. He is the inaugural Rector of the University Scholars Programme and founding Director of the East Asian Institute (1997–2007). He also served as Vice-Chancellor (President) of the University of Hong Kong (1986–1995). He began his teaching and academic career at the University of Malaya in Singapore and then in Kuala Lumpur. He has written on Chinese history and the history of overseas Chinese, and is the author of some 20 books including, most recently, his memoir, *Home is Not Here*.

YEO, George is a visiting scholar at Lee Kuan Yew School of Public Policy. He is Chairman and Executive Director of Kerry Logistics, member of the Kerry Holdings Board, and Independent Non-executive Director of AIA Group and Pinduoduo, and sits on the advisory boards of renowned institutions in Europe, the US and Asia. He had served in the Singapore Armed Forces, attaining the rank of Brigadier-General, and in the Ministry of Defence prior to entering politics. He was, variously, Minister of State for Finance and Minister for Information and the Arts, Health, Trade and Industry, and Foreign Affairs (1988–2011). He was appointed a member of the Pontifical Commission for Reference on the Economic-Administrative Structure of the Holy See in 2013 and became a member of the Vatican Council for the Economy in 2014.

Acknowledgements

IPS is grateful to the following organisations
for their support of Singapore Perspectives 2019.

TEMASEK

Acknowledgements